History & Memory
in German-Russian Country

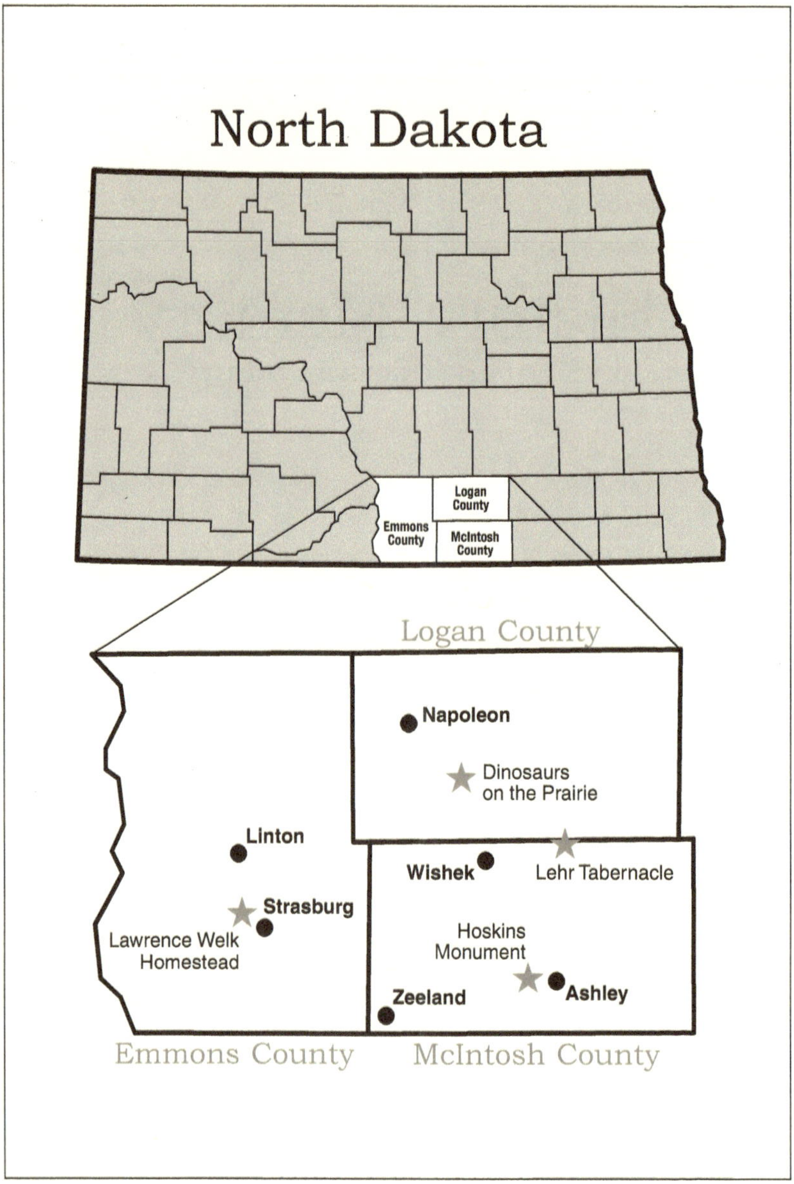

Heritage Guide Series
Volume 3

History & Memory

in German-Russian Country

Preface by Heritage Guide Series Editor
Thomas D. Isern

with essays by
Jessica Clark, Thomas D. Isern, Carol Just,
Debra Marquart, and Steve C. Martens

NDSU NORTH DAKOTA STATE UNIVERSITY PRESS

Fargo, North Dakota

Dept. 2576, P.O. Box 6050
Fargo, ND, 58108-6050
www.ndsupress.org

History & Memory in German-Russian Country
By Thomas D. Isern, Jessica Clark, Carol Just, Debra Marquart, and Steve Martens

First Edition
Second Printing

LCCN: 2025938197
ISBN: 978-1-946163-75-2

Cover and interior design by Deb Tanner
Cover photo by Suzzanne Kelley

The publication of *History & Memory in German-Russian Country* is made possible by the generous support of the Muriel and Joseph Richardson Fund, donors to the NDSU Press Fund and the NDSU Press Endowed Fund, and other contributors to NDSU Press.

Kimberly Wallin, Director
Suzzanne Kelley, Publisher
Kyle Vanderburg, Assistant Acquisitions Editor
Emma Borah, Graduate Research Assistant in Publishing
Sara Quiring and Brandon R. Stariha, Editorial Interns

Printed in the United States of America

Publisher's Cataloging-in-Publication
(Provided by Cassidy Cataloguing Services, Inc.)

Names: Isern, Thomas D. (Thomas Dean), 1952- editor, writer of preface. | Clark, Jessica (Jessica N.), contributor.
Title: History & memory in German-Russian country / preface by Heritage guide series editor Thomas D. Isern, with essays by Jessica Clark [and 4 others].
Other titles: History and memory in German-Russian country
Description: First edition. | Fargo, North Dakota : North Dakota State University Press, [2025] | Series: Heritage guide series (North Dakota State University Press) ; v. 3. | Includes bibliographical references and index.
Identifiers: ISBN: 9781946163752
Subjects: LCSH: Prairie Places Festival (2012 : Fargo, N.D.) | German Americans--North Dakota--History. | Germans--Russia--History. | Collective memory--North Dakota. | Agriculture--North Dakota. | North Dakota--History. | LCGFT: Essays. | Illustrated works. | BISAC: HISTORY / United States / State & Local / Midwest (IA, IL, IN, KS, MI, MN, MO, ND, NE, OH, SD, WI). | FAMILY & RELATIONSHIPS / Family History & Genealogy. | FAMILY & RELATIONSHIPS / Life Stages / General.
Classification: LCC: F645.G3 H57 2025 | DDC: 978.4800431--dc23

Contents

Preface

By the Heritage Guide Series Editor, Thomas D. Isern

Two section roads met somewhere in the middle of North Dakota, and this book is the result. One road is the longstanding path of North Dakota State's Institute for Regional Studies (founded in 1950, thus celebrating its seventy-fifth anniversary this year) toward the discovery and interpretation of the ethnic immigrant experience on the northern plains. Its publishing program, beginning in 1950 with titles published under the staid imprint, North Dakota Institute for Regional Studies, and continuing now under the enterprising imprint, North Dakota State University Press, has produced numerous volumes treating the Icelandic, Norwegian, German-Russian, German-Hungarian, and other ethnic histories of the region. Signal outposts on the path are William C. Sherman's *Prairie Mosaic: An Ethnic Atlas of Rural North Dakota* (1983, republished 2017), and the wonderfully encyclopedic volume in which also Father Bill had a shaping hand, *Plains Folk: North Dakota's Ethnic History* (1988).

The other road here intersecting originated with the establishment of the Center for Heritage Renewal as an agency of the institute in 2007, invested by the state board of higher education with a mission for historic preservation and heritage tourism. Founding director of the center, I also serve as series editor for the Heritage Guide Series published by North Dakota State University Press (NDSU Press). Moreover, the center has enjoyed a catalytic relationship with other NDSU partners—the Germans from Russia Heritage Center (under the visionary leadership of Michael M. Miller) and NDSU Extension—and with the people of south-central North Dakota in the operations of the Tri-County Tourism Alliance. The TCTA was established in 2010 to promote heritage tourism in German-Russian Country. Chief animators of this regional alliance have been two daughters of the country who hold NDSU Extension appointments therein—Carmen Rath Wald and Acacia Stuckle.

In 2012, when the future editor of NDSU Press, Dr. Suzzanne Kelley, was president of a statewide organization, Preservation North Dakota, she worked with a past president of PND—me—to bring the organization's annual meeting to Wishek, call it the Prairie Places Festival, and use it to encourage heritage exploration of German-Russian Country. The authors of chapters in this book all were plenary presenters at the 2012 meeting.

The Tri-County Tourism Alliance, having made substantial progress in the consciousness and branding of German-Russian Country, remains positively active, but the potential for heritage tourism in the region, although not a sleeping giant, remains less than fully awakened. Perhaps publication of this introductory guide (and, stay tuned for forthcoming volumes from NDSU Press documenting the heritage of the Germans from Russia) will help. Now, as for the content of the current work.

The disclamatory phrase that kept recurring when the oral historian Jessica Clark interviewed scores of German-Russian people of the land about their childhood was, "We didn't know any better." There was a professed innocence about their origins and upbringing, agreed-upon, rehearsed for the researcher who came out from the city. Their common stories touched on privation, busyness, persistence, and familial values. They made no place for recreation or fun. The interviewer, too, knows something about persistence, however, for after a pause, taking coffee and breaking bread, the interview resumes with greater relaxation, guard down, the shared authority that characterizes good oral history in the field asserting itself both ways. Certainly, the fuller German-Russian memory includes "great pride and care to reminiscence about their chores and responsibilities" but also allows there may have been some hijinks in the barn now and then. There appears still another, larger emergence, a refashioning, conscious or not, of German-Russian memory into a twenty-first-century German-Russian identity, even a sort of exceptionalism, formed by experience in place and the art of recollection.

We are privileged to travel with Dr. Clark, with all the authors of this anthology, and with all the Germans from Russia of whom they write, to the Lehr Tabernacle, where Clark told her story, and into the country of memory. Each literary contribution here brings its own lens to the land and people. For architectural historian Steve Martens that lens is material culture. His country of memory is filled with concrete things you can touch. He spoke of them in a great edifice of memory, within the fieldstone walls and under the long span arches of the Wishek Civic Center. His survey of New Deal 1930s construction projects spans the state of North Dakota but focuses on tropes and values embedded in the historic culture of the Germans from Russia. His essay, like the walls, evokes "Dust Bowl survival" and affirms "community and productive work as essential human values;" they may even "restore a spirit of hopefulness, worth and renewal."

"Examine the evidence with your own eyes," exhorts Martens, and "focus attention on some of these positive aspects of local culture here in German-Russian Country." Note the details of structure and of narrative: how, as recollected by stone mason Dan Rudolph, a pair of rock finishers working together would mark their names on the spot to be filed with the next stone, then cut it to exact need. Surely this told detail speaks of the material, but also of memory and of metaphor. For memory, too, is a structure of character and agency.

The oral lore and material culture of German-Russian Country appear, to the investigator looking in, exceptional, but the consciousness is absent—or perhaps just veiled. Debra Marquart, memoirist and daughter of the country, calls this "refusing nostalgia." Although only "vaguely aware" of something more when she was growing up in Logan County, Marquart nevertheless senses it in the jarred pickles and beets within the pantries and in the postures of paunchy old men. She investigates and finds grounding, perhaps even a Heimat, in the land itself. She finds a country strewn with graves and a narrative. She confronts the catalog of "North Dakota Sudden Deaths" left by one contributor to the WPA Writers Project files. She sits with the reality of "milk letters" from the old country surreptitiously disclosing continuing catastrophe in the old country, a tragedy so profound as to provoke self-imposed suppression of it, drawing a veil.

It is a veil pushed aside by another daughter of the land, Carol Just, who embraces the history, language, humor, song, and yes, pickles (even those pink watermelon pickles so formidable to visitors), plunging fully into the emerging German-Russian consciousness of the late twentieth century. Although descendant from those folk Bill Sherman in 1965 called "tight-knit and local," she becomes publicly evangelical in a cultural way. She prowls the prairie Heimat and becomes reinvested in the Andreas Gemeinde, St. Andrew's, her ancestral parish in the Beaver Creek district. She finds kinsmen willing to talk about her lineage, its trials and its triumphs. An assiduous researcher, she loves to tell the story. Perhaps she had to go away, and return, to become this way. But then, we are all, are we not, visitors in the land.

And fortunate to be so. Twenty-first-century Germans from Russia feel fortunate to be from the Russian Empire, now Ukraine, survivors of a blessedly timed diaspora that delivered them from the horrors of revolution, starvation, war, and persecution that would afflict the old country and be described in the milk letters. Today's expatriates from Ukraine, fleeing yet another exercise in tyranny, are caught in a transitional limbo between sovereignties so serious and extensive as to make the immigration troubles of our historic Germans from Russia (sometimes singled out for border delays on account of disease, but more broadly on account of nativism) seem relatively slight. On account of the situation in the old country today, we on the northern plains are once more isolated from ancestral sites in Ukraine.

After all the Journeys to the Homeland led by NDSU's Michael Miller to reconnect us with those sites, refreshing bittersweet ties across land and sea, we wonder if such journeys will be possible again in our lifetimes. At the time of the Prairie Places Festival in Wishek in 2012, those ties were on the rise. Even after Russia launched an invasion of Ukraine in 2014, once lines stabilized, the Journeys to the Homeland resumed. The next Russian invasion, in 2022, initiated a protracted war of attrition and severed the ties of ancestry and pilgrimage—perhaps for good.

Some of the Preservation North Dakota (PND) Prairie Festival attendees pose in front of the Old Settlers Monument. The picture includes Suzzanne Kelley, then president of PND and now editor in chief for NDSU Press, at the center of the photo. Some of the authors for this anthology are also present: Jessica Clark stands at the far left, Thomas D. Isern is in the back row just to the left of the monument, and Carol Just is at the immediate right of Suzzanne. *Photo by Ken Schmierer.*

Photo by Ken Schmierer.

The German-Russian survival on the northern plains and its emergent consciousness in late twentieth century, as described in the chapters to follow—where we see some folk drawing a veil, but others casting it down—are brought to a critical head by the course of events in the homeland. A tree cut off from its roots dies unless it has runners that grow and are tended where they are. This volume, then, is a gesture toward that sort of heritage husbandry. As we tend our orchard here, let us, who know our own history of struggle, lend both remembrance and assistance to those still embroiled in it.

Photo by Ken Schmierer.

German-Russian Country

By Thomas D. Isern[1]

[1]Thomas D. Isern is Professor of History & University Distinguished Professor at North Dakota State University. He is also one of the founders of the Tri-County Tourism Alliance, an organization promoting cultural tourism in Emmons, Logan, and McIntosh Counties, North Dakota. The resource base on which rests this introductory history of German-Russian Country comprises numerous secondary and published works, all of which are listed in the bibliography of this book. Wherever in this essay another, more specific document is referenced, it is footnoted.

In 1940, a United States government photographer, dispatched by the United States Department of Agriculture's Farm Security Administration, came to McIntosh County, North Dakota, to document the vitality of American life at the grassroots. Knowingly or not, the documentary artist had landed in German-Russian Country. One set of images by the photographer, John Vachon, depicted citizens, mainly men, deliberating and voting in McIntosh County's Beaver Creek Precinct. Another set of photos by Vachon documented the daily tasks of a farm woman, Mabel Bet-

Election committee, Beaver Creek precinct, McIntosh County, 1940. *Farm Security Administration image by John Vachon, courtesy Library of Congress.*

Mabel Bettenhausen with canned goods and produce in her cellar, McIntosh County, 1940. *Farm Security Administration image by John Vachon, courtesy Library of Congress.*

tenhausen—ironing clothes, baking bread, fueling the iron stove with corncobs, fetching potatoes from the cellar, and finally, contemplating the impressive rows of home-canned goods on the cellar shelves. Vachon might have titled his two series, *Some Things Change, Some Things Stay the Same.*[2]

The Germans from Russia are the largest ethnic immigrant group in North Dakota, and their impact on the culture and landscape of the northern plains is profound. German-Russian culture, dating from a settlement era in the 1880s, predominates in south-central North Dakota. Because of the hunger of the Ger-

[2]The nineteen Vachon photographs of the 1940 election in McIntosh County are available online from the Library of Congress: https://www.loc.gov/search/?fa=partof:lot+394. The fifteen Vachon photographs of Mrs. Bettenhausen and her household likewise are available: https://www.loc.gov/search/?fa=partof:lot+399.

man-Russians, an agricultural people, for land, their settlement culture also sprawls across north-central and western North Dakota and into the Prairie Provinces of Canada. Three counties in the German-Russian heartland of North Dakota—Emmons, Logan, and McIntosh—have come to refer to their region as German-Russian Country, recognizing the richness of their ethnic immigrant ancestry and encouraging travelers to explore it.

Who are the Germans from Russia? They are ethnic Germans who originated, historically, in the German-speaking principalities of central Europe and migrated, mostly during the late 1700s and early 1800s, into the Russian Empire. This was on invitation from the Russian government, which deployed the German settlers to occupy frontier lands and make them productive. In 1763, Catherine the Great famously invited foreigners, specifically Germans, to take up lands on the eastern Russian frontier. The Volga River valley was the main area to be developed by these settlers.[3] The success of this initiative led Czar Alexander I to issue another invitation in 1804, inviting Germans into districts recently wrested from Turkey.[4] These lands—rich lands with a moderate climate—lay along the Black Sea. Colonists from the southern German principalities traveled in wagon caravans for twenty weeks or more to take advantage of this opportunity.

Despite initial hardships, the Germans prospered in Russia for several generations. Their physical situation at first was difficult, but the political and economic terms of settlement were advantageous. Families received generous allocations of land—coincidentally, about the same amount per family as later would be offered by the Homestead Act in the United States. German colonies had their own local governments and courts. Their young men were exempted from conscription. They had their own schools,

---

[3]For an English translation of Catherine's 1763 manifesto, courtesy of the Center for Volga German Studies at Concordia University, see: "The Manifesto," https://www.volgagermans.org/history/manifesto.

[4]For a summary of points in Alexander's 1804 manifesto by a German-Russian historian, see "20 February 1804 Novaya Rossiya (Süd Rußland) Open for Settlement," https://www.germansfromrussiasettlementlocations.org/2018/02/20-february-1804-novaya-rossiya-sud.html.

retained their own language, and practiced their traditional faiths, with colonies organized along religious lines, homogenous as to Christian denomination.

Such advantages were not wasted on the German settlers, who built substantial and prosperous communities. They prided themselves on the replication and perpetuation of German culture in a distant land; indeed, some cultural historians say their culture, in a fashion common to isolated immigrant colonies, crystallized and hardened during the Russian interlude. On the other hand, the Germans also acquired Russian cultural traits, such as word-borrowings (*bashtan* means garden), culinary features (a *palatshinta* is a pumpkin turnover), and use of the Russian *troika* (a team of three horses drawing a carriage or sleigh). Certainly, too, they were affected by the land on which they lived and worked. They mastered not only the culture of small grains but also the raising of fruits and vegetables, and their livestock holdings were splendid, including the *rote Kuh*, the German red cow. They feared and fought the fierce Russian wolves, but they composed folksongs extolling the virtues of life on the land—“Wie schön ist das Ländliches Leben” (It’s Fine to Live Out in the Country) and “Kein schöner Land” (No Better Place than This).

Eventually the situation of the Germans in Russia was made precarious by the Russification policies of the late nineteenth century. In 1872 Alexander II revoked the Germans’ exemption from conscription. It also curtailed the Germans’ self-government and pressed them to use the Russian language in their schools. Such actions exacerbated growing economic and demographic pressures. With a growing population, there were not enough farms to go around. Such land as the Germans held was coveted, understandably, by Russian peasants, who had been freed from serfdom in 1861.

So the German-Russians began to emigrate to other lands, mainly to North America, and particularly to the Great Plains. Thus commenced what historians have come to call the “double diaspora” of the German-Russians. Nearly all of the German-Russian settlers in North Dakota are what is known as Schwarzmeerdeutschen, Black Sea Germans, meaning they came here from colonies near the Black Sea, mainly in what is now Ukraine. Their Atlantic departures would be from Hamburg and Bremen and other European ports, but their journeys began from various Black Sea districts, each with its own identity (still remembered by descendants now living in America). They hailed from the Grossliebenthal, Kutschurgan, Beresan, Glückstal, Hoffnungstal, Kronau-Orloff, and Berislaw districts, and from the province of Bessarabia. Early arrivals determined that the Dakota Territory offered them good opportunities, inasmuch as they required large amounts of open land.

Settlement of Dakota Territory by Germans from Russia, which began in 1873, first concentrated in the southeastern corner of the territory. As this locality filled with land-seekers, it became the staging area for expansion of German-Russian settlement into the central region of the territory. The town of Eureka, in a locality of present-day South Dakota first settled by

Photo (top) on p. 77, Spreading 'Hopper Bait at 6:00 A.M. on George Ritter Farm. *McIntosh County Extension Annual Reports, Institute for Regional Studies, North Dakota State University Archives.*

German-Russian farmer Jacob L. Raile and his Shorthorn bull, Vishek, 1940. *NDSU Extension 1939–1940 annual report for McIntosh County, Institute for Regional Studies, North Dakota State University Archives.*

German-Russians in 1884, emerged as a new entrepôt for the immigration with the arrival of the Milwaukee Railroad in 1887. The first Germans from Russia to settle in what is now North Dakota, however, made the wagon journey of more than two hundred miles from the town of Scotland in present-day South Dakota, in 1884. They founded St. John the Baptist Church, near present-day Zeeland, North Dakota.

The immigrant settlers of German-Russian Country almost all took up farming, many availing themselves of the provisions of the Homestead Act of 1862. Using its provisions, plus the pre-emption options of the earlier land laws, along with the Timber Culture Act of 1873, early settlers could acquire three quarters of land at minimal outright cost. Thus inspired, German-Russians streamed into northern Dakota Territory during the mid-1880s, even before the arrival of railroads. The extension of Northern Pacific, Milwaukee, and Soo Line railways spangled organized towns across German-Russian Country even as they consolidated and extended German-Russian farming settlement. While German-Russians pushed on to other parts of North Dakota and also into Canada during the late nineteenth and early twentieth centuries, the core of German-Russian Country—Emmons, Logan, and McIntosh Counties—largely filled up with these aspiring, industrious new Americans.

Their new homeland lay astride the Missouri Coteau, a land of rolling hills, grassy pastures, shining sloughs, and good, but not easy, farmland. The German-Russians integrated livestock into their farming operations, thus utilizing the resources offered by the land, and were more self-sufficient in their operations than most other settlers. They built homes of *batsa* brick, their own clay formed and dried into blocks, laid up in walls, and plastered with manure. They had big families and taught their children the virtues of hard work. When other work was not pressing, there always were rocks to pick—the everlasting residue of glacial till that had to be cleared by hand from fields and dragged onto piles. In time, innovative machine men Harley Brandner and James Bettenhausen would invent and manufacture the Wishek Disc, an implement that flexed to ride over rocks in the field.[5]

Because their settlements concentrated in particular localities, the Germans from Russia formed strong ethnic communities that stubbornly preserved their culture, a culture characterized by two traits: the German-Russians are an agricultural people, and they are a religious people. Generally, the western part of German-Russian Country (Emmons County and adjacent land) was settled by Roman Catholics and remains a Catholic stronghold today. Their parishes were, and are, largely served by Benedictines, with Father (later Bishop) Vincent Wehrle in the vanguard. Their parish schools were staffed by sisters of the Benedictine, Ursuline, and other orders. Their churches, such

---

[5]View the 1977 Brantner and Bettenhausen patent for the Pivotal Disc Gang Section of the Wishek Disc (US Patent 4,396,070) here: https://patentimages.storage.googleapis.com/d0/f5/d7/0766aacd8c77b2/US4396070.pdf.

German-Russian cemetery art: wrought iron grave marker in St. John the Baptist Cemetery, Emmons County.
Photo by Thomas D. Isern.

Pray for Peace Shrine housing Our Lady of Fatima statuary from St. Anthony Catholic Church, Logan County.
Photo by Thomas D. Isern.

as St. Mary's of Hague or Ss. Peter and Paul of Strasburg, are stately and ornate monuments to the faith. The eastern part of German-Russian Country (most of Logan and McIntosh Counties) was settled by various branches of Protestants, with strong tinges of evangelicalism and pietism. Congregations of German Lutherans quickly organized to provide religious continuity for the immigrants. Among the other Protestants, particularly notable were the efforts of the Evangelical Church, whose members built the Lehr Tabernacle in 1922.[6]

The Lehr Tabernacle has been the venue for religious revival meetings, often involving thousands of the faithful, from its building right down to today, and it is an architectural landmark of the first order. Indeed, the religious life of the German-Russians left enduring marks on the land that are wonders to present-day travelers. It is the great Catholic churches that draw the most attention, but others are equally compelling. Consider, for example, St. Andrew's Lutheran Church, near Zeeland. This relic parish preserves not only a lovely wood-frame church dating from 1906 but also its predecessor, a stone and gumbo vernacular building dating from 1892.[7]

Shrines are common in association with churches, but German-Russians also have a penchant for exhibiting their faith across the landscape. The wrought iron crosses crafted as grave markers by German-Russian blacksmiths are fascinating works of folk art filling many German-Russian cemeteries.[8] Roadside shrines built by German-Russian faith communities, such as the Prairie Bells & Grotto of the Holy Family, established by the Vetter family, are common. The Pray for Peace Shrine preserves the Our Lady of Fatima statuary once housed by a rural church. On their

---

[6]Carolyn Schott, "The Lehr Tabernacle," *Heritage Review* 37, no. 1 (March 2007): 11–18.

[7]Nomination of St. Andrew's Lutheran Church to the National Register of Historic Places (US Department of the Interior, National Park Service), 1990, https://catalog.archives.gov/id/75326584.

[8]The foundational research on German-Russian wrought iron crosses is in Timothy J. Kloberdanz, "Cross-makers: German-Russian Folk Specialists of the Great Plains," PhD dissertation, Indiana University, 1986, copy in the Germans from Russia Heritage Collection, North Dakota State University Libraries.

farm near Braddock, Pete and Mary Ellen Naaden have emplaced a sobering crucifix made by renowned metal artist Tom Neary. Visitors to German-Russian Country should sense that they are traversing a sacred landscape.

Visitors also have the opportunity to enjoy traditional German-Russian cuisine, which features, more than anything else, dough in various manifestations! Knoephle (spelling varies), ribbele, strudels, noodles, and dumplings abound. The German-Russian dessert known as Kuchen, a particular favorite across the region, features a custard-like filling, often including fruit or cottage cheese, on a thin yeast dough. *Fleischküchle*, meat-filled fried pies, may be found for sale alongside hamburgers at a drive-in. Watermelon pickles made not from the rind, but from the pink flesh of the melon, confound the uninitiated. Arguments burst out spontaneously over the relative virtues of the *Wascht* (sausage), head cheese, bologna, or summer sausage dispensed by this local meat locker versus that one. Purists gather annually in their garages to mix pork with venison to produce their own Wascht the way they remember the old folks doing it. While doing so they may sample the traditional schnapps of the German-Russians, known colloquially as red-eye, flavored with caramel and anise. German-Russians still tend their bashtan and, in the fashion illustrated by Mrs. Bettenhausen, preserve their produce, wholesomeness and thrift being complementary virtues.

There was a time, beginning with the settlement era and continuing through the two world wars of the twentieth century, when German-Russian identity was an ambivalent thing. In her memoir, *Along the Trails of Yesterday*, Nina Farley Wishek (not herself a German-Russian), while praising the industry of the Germans from Russia, nevertheless portrays them with a sense of local color that is a bit patronizing. She features young German-Russian women in a chapter titled, “Maids I Have Known.” Monsignor George Aberle recalls the disparagements of what Anglo-Americans called “Russian” immigrants and counters by calling them "builders of an empire" and "great heroes of the past." Still, the dean of North Dakota historians, Elwyn Robinson, feels compelled to disparage German-Russians as clannish, illiterate, and anti-education—disparagements conclusively rebutted by Jessica Clark in her oral history of the Germans from Russia.

By the 1970s, a time of rising ethnic consciousness across the United States, Germans from Russia were ready to proclaim and own their lineage. The opening salvo came from a young priest with German-Russian parishioners—William C. Sherman—who delivered a pathbreaking paper, "The Germans from Russia," at the 1965 symposium on the Great Plains convened by the Institute for Regional Studies, North Dakota State University.

Lawence Welk descendant Gerard Schwab harvesting wheat on the historic Ludwig and Christina Welk Homestead, Emmons County, 2014. *Photo by Thomas D. Isern.*

Struck by the intercontinental scope of German-Russian history, impressed by the cultural persistence of the Germans who had come to Dakota, and eager to bring them into the burgeoning scholarly literature in regional ethnic studies, Father Bill devised a better, more descriptive phrase to describe them: the Germans from Russia. Soon after landmark works of German-Russian history such as those by George Rath and Joseph Height appeared in print. The Germans from Russia Heritage Society, a popular organization dedicated to the preservation of German-Russian history and culture, was founded in Bismarck in 1971 and publishes a historical journal, the *Heritage Review*. The Germans from Russia Heritage Collection (GHRC) of North Dakota State University provides academic support for cultural preservation through public programming and by maintaining a comprehensive research collection of German-Russian materials. The GRHC has collaborated with Prairie Public (statewide public broadcasting) in the production of award-winning documentaries, including *The Germans from Russia: Children of the Steppe, Children of the Prairie*. In 2011, recognizing the rich cultural resources extant in south-central North Dakota, representatives of local communities, NDSU Libraries, NDSU Extension, and the NDSU Center for Heritage Renewal organized the Tri-County Tourism Alliance to promote Emmons, Logan, and McIntosh Counties as German-Russian Country.

Now powerfully aware of their status as a *Volk auf dem Land*, a distinctive people of the land, German-Russian farmers still plant and harvest, German-Russian faithful still gather for worship, German-Russian cooks still feed their families, and German-Russian communities remain vital—sustained by history and memory in German-Russian Country.

Oral historian Jessica Clark, backed by an honor board of German-Russian evangelicals, addresses the Prairie Places Festival in the Lehr Tabernacle. *Photo by Ken Schmierer.*

The Lehr Tabernacle, with its distinctive octagonal skylight and bracing, a major religious site dating from 1922.
Photo by Ken Schmierer.

The Landscape of Memory in German-Russian Country

By Jessica Clark[1]

[1]Jessica Clark, one of the first graduates in the North Dakota State University Department of History PhD program, is now Provost and Vice President of Academic Affairs at Bellevue College, Washington. Her essay is rooted in the presentation she made in the Lehr Tabernacle, Lehr, North Dakota, for the 2012 Preservation North Dakota Conference.

On a windy day in July 2005, the late Emil E. Schaffer of Gackle, North Dakota accompanied an oral history team on a landmark walk, which included a tour of his grandparents' old house, a house that was built in 1891 in rural south-central North Dakota.[2] While Emil did not have extensive memories of this specific house, seeing its architectural design and experiencing the lively summer weather stirred his memories. For instance, the house's deep windowsills triggered his memories of sitting in similar windows as a child in his own home. Being inside this decrepit house on a warm but windy day also reminded him of how effective sod was at regulating temperatures, keeping the house cool during summers and warm during winters. Emil reminisced about the architectural design of sod houses, comparing his grandparents' "mud house" to his parents' "sod house." This landmark walk, although continuously interrupted by loud gusts of wind, provided a deeper insight into the life, memories, and identity of Emil E. Schaffer.[3]

Born and reared in rural, south-central North Dakota, during the early 1900s, Emil is just one of many German-Russians who volunteered or agreed to participate in an oral history project designed "to preserve the history and heritage of the second- and third-generation Germans from Russia."[4] Created in 2005, the Dakota Memories Oral History (Dakota Memories) preserved the "childhood memories and family relationships" of German-Rus-

---

[2]The oral history team consisted of my husband, Dr. Will Clark, and me. At that time, my husband was serving as the lead videographer and photographer for the Dakota Memories Oral History Project.
[3]Emil E. Schaffer, interview by Jessica Clark, July 18, 2005, DVD, Dakota Memories Oral History Project [hereafter referred to as Dakota Memories], Germans from Russia Heritage Collection, North Dakota State University Libraries, Fargo, North Dakota.
[4]Schaffer interview; "Dakota Memories Oral History Project," last modified October 31, 2012, accessed January 12, 2013, http://library.ndsu.edu/grhc/dakotamemories/home.html.

Emil E. Schaffer visiting his grandparents' abandoned homestead during a landmark walk with Drs. William H. Clark and Jessica Clark. *Photograph by Jessica Clark. Photograph courtesy of the Dakota Memories Oral History Project, Germans from Russia Heritage Collection, North Dakota State University Libraries.*

sians on the Northern Plains.[5] After collecting nearly two hundred oral histories, organizers of this project discovered that these interviews revealed a new landscape of memory for the descendants of German-Russians. By employing a variety of oral history techniques, like the landmark and cemetery walks, Dakota Memories oral historians discovered that the second- and third-generation

[5]Dakota Memories.

German-Russians have a new, complex story. Their reconstructed narrative—the new German-Russian story—is a story of hardships as well as happiness.

The narrative of most (not all, but most) German-Russian descendants interviewed for the project begins with their ancestors migrating to the Black Sea region of South Russia in the mid-1700s, at the invitation of Tsarina Catherine the Great.[6] These immigrants were looking for new opportunities, which the tsarina promised, along with free land and autonomy in Russia. According to German-Russian scholar Renate Birdenthal, Germans from Russia "were land-hungry farmers, who, in 1763, accepted the Enlightenment-influenced invitation of German-born Tsarina Catherine the Great of Russia to settle hitherto uncultivated land and to model modern agricultural techniques to surrounding peasants."[7] Germans in Russia prospered, until the Russian government began reneging on the promises of Catherine the Great and implementing a policy of *Russification* (nearly one hundred years after the initial invitation). Around the same time, mid-1800s, information regarding the opportunity for free land in America under the Homestead Act of 1862 started circulating through Russia. As a result, thousands of Germans left Russia, forging "a new, self-conscious ethnic group—Germans from Russia."[8]

The migration patterns of these Black Sea German-Russians in America and Canada reveal the trials and tribulations this ethnic group experienced in search of a new homeland.

> In the early 1900s, for instance, thousands of Germans from Russia moved from the Sauerkraut Triangle (a small enclave of Germans from Russia in north-central South Dakota and south-central

[6]Jessica Clark, "Germans from Russia on the Northern Plains: An Oral History Project" [hereafter referred to as Clark, "Germans from Russia on the Northern Plains] (PhD diss., North Dakota State University, 2010), 9–11.

[7]Renate Birdenthal, "Reaching Out: The Double Diaspora of Germans from Russia" (paper presented at the *Heimat Abroad*: The Boundaries of Germanness, New York University, 1999).

[8]Clark, "Germans from Russia on the Northern Plains," 10.

> North Dakota) to western North Dakota and north-central North Dakota, creating the German-Russian Triangle. Some also continued their migration across the 49th parallel.[9]

According to their established narrative, German-Russians continued to move from South Dakota into North Dakota (as well as Saskatchewan) because of their continuous hardships—poor farmland, droughts, infestations, lack of opportunities, etcetera. Thus, the ethnic group's identity began rooted in the hardships of Germany and Russia and was solidified by their trials in America and Canada.

In the 1960s and 1970s, with the passing of many first-generation immigrants, German-Russians began to preserve their ethnic group's collective memory. These cultural insiders (members of the ethnic group) started by creating societies and organizations devoted to the preservation of their ethnic identity. In addition, scholars from within the ethnic group, like Shirley Fischer Arends, George Rath, and Richard Sallet, wrote and published books dedicated to the group's collective memory. These insider societies and accounts are invaluable to the formation of the German-Russian narrative and identity.[10]

In 2005, Michael M. Miller (a second-generation Black Sea German-Russian and Emeritus Director of the Germans from Russia Heritage Collection), Dr. Tom Isern (University Distinguished Professor and Professor of History) and I (now Provost and Vice President of Academic Affairs, then a doctoral student) launched Dakota Memories in an attempt to preserve the childhood memories of German-Russian descendants. From 2005 through 2010, oral historians for this project interviewed 199 men and women from South Dakota to Saskatchewan, with the majority of narrators located in North Dakota. This collaborative project coordinated by both insiders and outsiders (those of Ger-

[9]Clark, "Germans from Russia on the Northern Plains," 11.
[10]Clark, "Germans from Russia on the Northern Plains,"13.

man-Russian descent and those not of German-Russian descent) focused on the descendants' collective memory and identity, and as a result, uncovered a new story, a reconstructed story.

The project's trained oral historians were able to tap into the deep memories of their narrators because of their methodology. Dakota Memories oral historians conducted most interviews on the home turf of narrators, and they devoted at least a full day to each narrator (sometimes more). This process permitted narrators time to become familiar with the oral history teams, which consisted of an oral historian and videographer. In "Using Oral History for a Family History Project," oral historian Linda Shopes writes "an interview is above all a social interaction."[11] In other words, the more at ease a narrator and oral historian feel, the more engaged and productive the interview. Given the focus of this project (as well as limitations of the recording devices) the Dakota Memories oral historians conducted most interviews on a two-to-one basis—an oral historian, videographer, and narrator. This arrangement limited the external influences present during each oral history.[12]

Then again, it is not entirely possible to remove all external influences. Dakota Memories oral historians scheduled their residencies (trips to the field to conduct oral histories) a month or more in advance, which permitted narrators plenty of time to prepare for the interview process. Preparations officially included completing and submitting a biography form and a topic checklist (selecting the topics to be discussed during the oral history process), organizing photos, and more. Unofficially, it involved many conversations with family and friends. Narrators were drafting the official (or superficial) narrative by sharing their memories among themselves, establishing or revisiting their ethnic group's story.

[11]Linda Shopes, "Using Oral History for a Family History Project," in *Oral History: An Interdisciplinary Anthology*, edited by David K. Dunaway and Willa K. Baum (New York: AltaMira Press, 1996), 234.

[12]For more information on external influences and the relationship between an oral historian and a narrator, review Michael Frisch, *A Shared Authority: Essays on the Craft and Meaning of Oral and Public History* (New York: State University of New Press 1990).

For some this was intentional, for others it was happenstance. Regardless, they were rehearsing their stories. Hence the importance of the Dakota Memories methodology, as it allowed oral historians to break through the established collective memory and into unrehearsed deep memories. And, to the surprise of both oral historians and narrators, these memories unmasked a new landscape of memory among the German-Russian descendants.

Dakota Memories oral historians were trained to conduct traditional sit-down interviews, as well as photo album tours, memory maps, cooking and musical demonstrations, and landmark and cemetery walks. The techniques not only helped narrators move past their collective narrative, but they also helped them forget about the intimidating video camera recording their interview.[13] The various techniques were memory triggers—triggers used to delve deeper into the history of German-Russians. By evoking one (or more) of the five senses (sight, sound, smell, taste, and touch), Dakota Memories oral historians triggered memories that were not revealed during the traditional sit-down oral histories.

The landmark and cemetery walk were especially important in revealing this new landscape of memory in German-Russian country. Landmark walks triggered memories of the environment (nature and weather), family (relationships), chores, school (grade school and high school), and religious devotion; whereas cemetery walks triggered memories of family (relationships), religious devotion, death (funerals), and healthcare. These techniques were not used during every interview. They were only employed typically after a sit-down interview and if narrators were willing and able. For the most part, narrators who participated in the walks dove deeper into their stories, revealing memories they had not anticipated sharing.

Rooted in tradition, but altered to accommodate new experiences, these deep memories of the second- and third-generation

[13]For more information on the special techniques employed by Dakota Memories oral historians, please review Clark, "Germans from Russia on the Northern Plains," xx.

German-Russians created a new (or reconstructed) story. Their story can be summed up with a saying that was repeated in some fashion by most narrators—*We didn't know any better!* Reflecting on their past, these memory-makers began altering their ethnic group's traditional story of hardships by recounting stories of happiness and bliss, stories of the good times. This new story is "rooted in an ancestral past with tales of trials and tribulations, and shaped by childhood experiences and memories, as well as present conditions."[14] It is a complex story, "reflective of both generational change and ethnic resilience."[15]

Memories of the northern plains environment shared during the Dakota Memories oral histories are reflective of this new identity. The environment was one of the most discussed topics during the process, especially during landmark and cemetery walks. Often, discussions unfolded (or started) about the unpredictable nature of the current weather patterns, which in turn evoked memories about the weather and environmental extremes witnessed growing up on the plains. On windy days narrators reminisced about the wind; on chilly days, narrators reflected on winters; and on warm days narrators shared stories of summers. In other words, the environment itself was a memory trigger. During the traditional sit-down interview, most narrators focused on the trying and terrifying experiences, such as prairie fires, dust storms, grasshopper invasions, blizzards, and climate. Yet, during the walks, especially the landmark walks, narrators often reminisced about their tranquil experiences, like roaming fields, climbing trees, picking berries, hunting deer, and trapping gophers.

Narrators reminisced about the environment because it had a direct impact—socially, culturally, and physically—on them. Although most interviews took place during the summer months on warm and windy days, walking through fields, driving on long dirt roads, visiting schools and churches evoked memories of

[14]Clark, "Germans from Russia on the Northern Plains," xxxi.
[15]Clark, "Germans from Russia on the Northern Plains," xxxi.

all seasons. First and foremost, narrators spent a great deal of time discussing summer and winter. Undoubtedly, summer is discussed at great length because most of the interviews took place during summer months. Yet, this season also allowed narrators an opportunity to perpetuate their tale of hardship. With time and the right questions, narrators also reminisced about the opportunities afforded to them during the dry and warm season. Winter was the second most discussed season. And, like summer, narrators initially focused on the stories that aligned with their accepted narrative—stories of perseverance. Once the deep memories started surfacing, narrators revealed that they also found time for winter pastime activities. Fall and spring were the two seasons usually avoided until some prodding by oral historians. Narrators tended to associate fall with harvests and school. Rarely was it discussed as a favorite season. When spring was discussed, narrators emphasized a refreshing and rejuvenating time of year—the time of year when the environment thawed.[16]

Most narrators of the Dakota Memories grew up during an era historians have dubbed as the Dirty Thirties. The 1930s on the northern plains (as well as much of the Great Plains) was a time of an economic depression and a natural catastrophe—a severe drought. Countless narrators, as a result, have vivid memories of this era. Robert R. Gab of Eureka, South Dakota, for instance, shared his childhood memories of dust storms and insect infestations with oral historian Cassie Ptacek in 2008. Born in 1926, Robert was a young child during the thirties. Yet, the events of this decade are ingrained in his memory and his ethnic group's collective memory. He remembered the world turning dark as wall clouds of dirt made their way through the small town of Hillsview, South Dakota. Until his younger siblings were born (siblings who were nearly ten years his junior), Robert was his

[16]For more information on the environment, see "'Amber Waves': The Northern Plains Environment" in Clark, "Germans from Russia on the Northern Plains," 22–65.

"mother's maid."[17] And, as such, Robert described the effort to clean a house following a dust storm as "massive."[18] According to Robert, anytime a dust storm rolled into the area they quickly closed up the house, wetted towels for the cracks and crevices, and waited for it to blow over. Then, despite their efforts, they had an incredible amount of dust and dirt to clean out of the house. This left "quite an impression on me," Robert insisted.[19]

During his interview, Robert also recounted his grandfather's funeral, which took place in the late spring one year during this disastrous decade. During the funeral procession from the church to the grave site, Robert remembered having people placed between each car in an effort to prevent them from colliding. Apparently, the dirt was so thick it was impossible "to see the car in front of you."[20] It was the responsibility of the people in between the cars to warn drivers of collision risks by tapping on the hoods. Nonetheless, like most narrators, Robert remembered that even though the Dirty Thirties were hard, he had time to play. On one occasion, he recalled getting really excited while playing outside because he noticed some rain clouds approaching. He ran inside and reported to his parents "we are going to get rain!"[21]

Robert R. Gab's story is just one of many that reflect the negative and the positive experiences German-Russian descendants had interacting with the environment as children on the northern plains. Over time, Dakota Memories narrators were reconstructing their ethnic identity to accommodate their childhood experiences. Their reconstructed story is undoubtedly rooted in their traditional narrative of the terrifying effects of the Great Depression, but they coexisted with the memories of their tranquil experiences. This reconstruction was made possible largely because American- and Canadian-born German-Russians have no basis of environmental comparison. In fact, their childhood expe-

---

[17]Robert R. Gab, interview by Cassie Ptacek, May 15, 2005, DVD, Dakota Memories.
[18]Ibid.
[19]Ibid.
[20]Ibid.
[21]Ibid.

riences mirror the experiences of others on the plains during the twentieth century—neither all bad, nor all good. Thus, their story had to change.[22]

Landmark and cemetery walks were wonderful for revealing new and more detailed stories about family relationships. Narrators of the Dakota Memories primarily discussed three types of family relationships: grandparent-grandchild, parent-child, and sibling-sibling. It was not uncommon for narrators to take their oral history teams to the gravesites of their late grandmothers, only to find themselves sharing memories of tasty dough dishes. Narrators also took their oral historian and videographer to their parents' homestead, where they revealed stories about their fathers making them labor endlessly in the field. On visits to the one-room schoolhouses, narrators shared stories of siblings coaxing them into mischief.

Memories of familial relationships revealed that through these relationships narrators were not only remembering their ethnic history and identity; they were reshaping it as well. In other words, even as children, these German-Russian descendants were blending their past with their present. Their intergenerational relationships, combined with the fact that most German-Russians lived in ethnic communities, aided in their strong connection to tradition and heritage. Their generational relationships, including the relationships formed by attending public schools, permitted them an opportunity to change. For German-Russian descendants, grandparents were repositories of memories (a place to learn about the group's history and heritage), parents were instructors of discipline and hard work (a place to learn about the morals and values of the group), and siblings were co-conspirators in creating new experiences (a place to reconstruct or modernize the group's narrative).[23]

---

[22]Clark, "Germans from Russia on the Northern Plains," 22–65.

[23]For more information on the familial relationships, see "'More than a Photo': Familial Relationships" in Clark, "Germans from Russia on the Northern Plains," 66–97.

For example, Christina Rose Maria (Bast) Krismer, born in 1937 in rural Saskatchewan, has many fond memories of her distant and close familial relationships. During her oral history, Christina took the lead oral historian (the author) to a remote, small-town cemetery: Sedley Cemetery in Sedley, Saskatchewan. Buried in this cemetery are Christina's great-grandparents, grandparents, and parents. Although Christina has limited-to-no personal memories of her great-grandparents, during the cemetery walk she visited the gravesites of her great-grandparents, John and Anna Maria Bast. While at their gravesites, Christina vaguely remembered her great-grandfather's funeral. If she recalls correctly, he passed when she was barely five years old. Her great-grandmother, however, passed before, and Christina has no recollection of her. Thinking back to her great-grandfather's funeral, she remembered his body was kept in her home for some time. Her memory of people carrying the casket from her house and loading it onto a buggy harnessed to horses is ingrained.[24]

Familial relationships, regardless of the type or length, played a key role in the formation and maintenance of identity. Christina had limited memories of her great-grandparents—memories that reflected traditions, not heritage. She learned her heritage from her grandparents, who shared stories with her about her great-grandparents immigrating to Canada. These stories allowed her to identify with people within her ethnic group. As she stated, while standing next to the gravesites of her distant relatives, she may have limited recollections of these people, but they are part of her story, they are a part of her history. Christina, through her participation in this oral history project, as well as through her scrapbooks, reconstructed her family's narrative. She, as other narrators did, preserved the traditional story of the first generation, as well as the new story of her generation.[25] These oral histories embraced the bad with the good, blended the past with the

[24]Christina Rose Maria (Bast) Krismer, interview by Jessica Clark, July 28, 2006, DVD, Dakota Memories.

[25]Krismer, interview, July 28, 2006.

present. Through this project, participants reconstructed their narrative; they recorded the new German-Russian story.[26]

Regardless of the generation—first, second, or third—German-Russians take great pride and care to reminisce about their chores and responsibilities. This element of childhood easily reinforced the traditional narrative of hardships and perseverance. Dakota Memories narrators, without hesitation, answered questions about engaging in pastime activities with: *We didn't have time for fun. There was too much work to be done.* Many narrators even referenced the saying *Arbeiten macht Lieben Süß* or *Work makes life sweet.* Their memories of milking cows, separating milk, hauling hay, picking rocks, ironing laundry, and baking bread align with their ancestors' story of having a hard life. Initially, Dakota Memories narrators emphasized stories of these dreary chores and stern responsibilities. After time, deeper inquiry, and some special interview techniques, however, they revealed the complexities of their childhood.

In reality, German-Russian children labored no more than other farm children from the era. Parents, regardless of their ethnicity, used chores and responsibilities as educational opportunities. By assigning children chores, parents were providing their children with practical experience and socialization. In addition, for many families during the 1930s having their children work (especially on farms) was an economic necessity. As most Dakota Memories narrators insist, they were expected to work hard, but it was not abuse or neglect. In fact, as the oral historians began posing questions or embarked upon landmark walks, narrators began to acknowledge that working hard as a youth actually provided them with vast opportunities and memorable life experiences.[27]

On a warm, spring day in May 2008, for example, oral historian Eric Mischnick escorted Betty (Krueger) Brosz of Fredonia,

---

[26]Clark, "Germans from Russia on the Northern Plains," 66–97.

[27]For more information on the chores and responsibilities, see "'Work Makes Life Sweet': Chores and Responsibilities," in Clark, "Germans from Russia on the Northern Plains," 98–125.

The Milk Maids. Left to right: Frieda, Dee, Emma, and Ruth Korus. *Photograph courtesy of the Dakota Memories Oral History Project, Germans from Russia Heritage Collection, North Dakota State University Libraries.*

North Dakota, on a landmark walk. With birds chirping and the sun shining, Betty shared an atypical account of growing up on the northern plains. One might call her oral history nostalgic. At one point during the walk, Eric asked Betty to recount her memories of chores as a child. Grinning from ear-to-ear, Betty insisted that "farm life was a good, clean life."[28] The first chore that came to mind was milking cows. As with most Dakota Memories narrators, milking cows was a twice daily chore. During the traditional sit-down interview, most narrators discuss the monotonous nature of milking cows. Yet, Betty, on this landmark walk, decided to reveal some little enjoyments that could be found in this daily chore. Betty found great pleasure in pail feeding the milk to young calves. She also enjoyed squirting milk straight from the cows' udders into her kittens' mouths. There was fun to be had on a farm, insisted Betty.

Of course, not every chore was enjoyable. Betty remembered cleaning the cream separator as quite tedious. She is not exactly sure why she disliked this chore so much—other than it was another one of those daily chores. She also remembered that it was a long process. According to her narrative, her sister usually went inside to clean the house, while she stayed outside to clean the separator. By the time she finished cleaning the separator, her sister had the entire house cleaned. For Betty, cleaning the separator was her least favorite chore.

In addition to cleaning the house and producing food (i.e., milking cows and separating the milk), Betty also recounted her memories of helping with the field work. Growing up in a household with three siblings (one sister and two brothers), Betty often found herself out in the field, as well as in the house. "There was no hired hand," she insisted.[29] Her father believed there was no need to hire someone when there were able-bodied children on the farm. The Krueger children had experience shocking bundles, raking hay, and much more. But, as Betty recalled, "it was

[28]Betty (Krueger) Brosz, interview by Eric Mischnick, May 29, 2008, DVD, Dakota Memories

[29]Brosz, interview, May 29, 2008.

good work."[30] This work provided children with "fresh air" and "good exercise."[31] She insisted that back then people did not need *Curves* for exercise.[32]

Betty's memories of chores reaffirmed the saying *Work makes life sweet.* Memories regarding chores and responsibilities tend to showcase the ethnic group's resilience. Times may have been tough for German-Russian descendants growing up in the 1930s. Yet, by working hard, supporting each other, and living off the land, they survived. These stories allow the second- and third-generation German-Russians to perpetuate the established narrative. However, the stories rarely stopped there. During most Dakota Memories oral histories, narrators were encouraged to reveal their individual stories. With these individual memories emerged a story that intertwined the bitter and the sweet. This new story is multi-dimensional and complex, a narrative that attempts to bridge the ancestral hardships with personal experiences.[33]

Although narrators rarely intended to reveal memories that complicated their stories, many topics made this inevitable—such as school. Most narrators chose to reminisce about one-room schoolhouses, country schoolteachers, grade school and high school curricula, recesses, noon-hours, and more. Memories of this institution reveal that schools were established as agents of acculturation. They promoted assimilation—Americanization and Canadianization. Yet, the oral histories also reveal that these institutions did more than just acculturate and assimilate. In rural America and Canada, one-room schoolhouses also reinforced the memory and identity of ethnic enclaves. They brought children together, which provided opportunities (no matter how small) for children to perpetuate their ethnic heritage. In other words, just

---

[30]Brosz, interview, May 29, 2008.
[31]Ibid.
[32]Ibid.
[33]Clark "Germans from Russia on the Northern Plains," 98-125.

like the German-Russian identity, secular schools in these ethnic communities were complex.[34]

Marlene Ann (Kraft) Smith is one of the youngest Dakota Memories participants. She became a narrator for the project after inviting a team to interview her father—the only first-generation German-Russian interviewed for the Dakota Memories project. Upon completion of the interview, Marlene agreed to share her story of growing up in the 1940s. During her landmark walk, Marlene stumbled onto some old *Dick and Jane* textbooks. She reminisced about how students learned English in the country schools through the readers. While she did not have a copy of the first set of readers, she recalled it being very simplistic: "See Dick. See Jane. See Spot."[35] Then, Marlene points out, the book progressed, getting increasingly harder, until kids were reading full-length stories. Marlene feels truly blessed to have saved these readers from her old schoolhouse. She has fond memories of using them, as well as ink-wells and pens. She loved school.[36]

Most narrators shared fond memories of attending school. A few incorporated stories that aligned with their traditional narrative. Some shared stories about being held out of school to work on the farm, or stories about being forced to abandon the German language for the English or French language, or stories about being denied the chance to attend high school. However, these stories rarely overshadowed the positive memories narrators shared, stories of playing at recess, learning about reading, writing, and arithmetic, and forming life-long friendships with children from within the ethnic group.

The stories recounted reveal that immigrant children played an active role in maintaining their ethnic identity. Although schools were set up as agents of acculturation and assimilation, German-Russian children did not let that destroy their identity.

---

[34]For more information country schools, see "Reading, Writing, and Arithmetic: Grade School" in Clark, "Germans from Russia on the Northern Plains," 126–62.

[35]Marlene Ann (Kraft) Smith, interview by Cassie Ptacek, June 15, 2007, DVD, Dakota Memories.

[36]Smith, interview, June 15, 2007.

Students who attended Feska School No. 3 [Alma is on the far right in the back row]. *Alma (Janke) Schott, photograph courtesy of the Dakota Memories Oral History Project, Germans from Russia Heritage Collection, North Dakota State University Libraries.*

In reality, schools appear to be more agents of cultural diffusion than assimilation. They aimed at teaching children national values, but by bringing children from within one ethnic group together, they were tempering the ethnic identity. Germans from Russia were becoming American German-Russians and Canadian German-Russians depending on their locale. This group was resilient.[37]

Religious devotion was also a topic discussed often during the sit-down interviews, as well as during landmark and cemetery walks. It was quite common for Dakota Memories oral historians to accompany narrators on tours of local churches and

[37]Clark, "Germans from Russia on the Northern Plains," 126–62.

cemeteries. Since religion was such an integral part of growing up German-Russian, most narrators selected this topic from the onset. A wealth of stories is preserved by the Dakota Memories project about church services and programs, like baptisms, first communions, confirmations, weddings, and funerals. Church was an institution that not only permitted the maintenance of ethnic identity, but in many ways encouraged it. It was also a safe place to absorb change. Thus, many second- and third-generation German-Russians found that church was the perfect place to blend their new culture with their ethnic identity. In essence, they used this institution to refashion their story.[38]

Wilfred Jacob Boechler of Allen, Saskatchewan, spent nearly an hour reminiscing about his religious devotion inside the Catholic Church in his hometown. He had already spent a great deal of time discussing it during his sit-down interview, as well. For Wilfred, being Catholic was just as much a part of his identity as being German-Russian, if not more so. He had fond memories of midnight Mass and church services. During his oral history, he not only described the church in great detail; he also recited (in Latin) some scriptures he was taught as a Mass Server. For Wilfred church was a place to be a German-Russian boy in Canada. There were no expectations of talking solely English or German, because Masses were in Latin.[39]

Regardless of the denomination—Catholic or Protestant—church services fostered neither assimilation nor acculturation. Church was an institution that permitted people, including German-Russian children, to blend their national identity with their ancestral heritage. It did not favor one over the other. For many children, like Wilfred, church became a central place to process conflicting ideas, while at the same time to learn about the spiritual world around them. Thus, these children were agents of change

---

[38]For more information on religious devotion, see "'*Gott ist die Liebe*': Religious Devotion" in Clark, "Germans from Russia on the Northern Plains," 198–232.

[39]Wilfred Jacob Boechler, interview by Jessica Clark, July 23, 2006, DVD, Dakota Memories.

Delores (Kuhn) Becker with Betty and Barbara Kuhn during their first Holy Communion. *Becker photo 6, courtesy of the Dakota Memories Oral History Project, Germans from Russia Heritage Collection, North Dakota State University Libraries.*

and the church was a place of tradition. Church was a place that allowed for the absorptions of American and Canadian ideas.[40]

We didn't know any better sums up the childhood memories of German-Russian descendants on the northern plains. Countless narrators used this saying at points within their narrative, to justify their new story. By reciting these or similar words, German-Russian descendants were aligning their memories with the established story of their ethnic group—the story of hardship and oppression. The Dakota Memories project, however, has revealed the complexity of memory among the second- and third-generation German-Russians. It shows that this new landscape of memory in German-Russian Country consists of two spheres of memory: the collective and the individual. Unbeknownst to the narrators themselves, they were telling two tales: a story of oppression and hardship and a story of fun and enjoyment. The emergence of the new story reveals that German-Russians themselves were responsible for constructing their narrative, and as a result, their identity. Thus, those who participated in the Dakota Memories reshaped the group's narrative.[41]

To illustrate the complexity of the new German-Russian story, we can examine the interview with Emil Roesler, who was born and reared in Lehr, North Dakota, in the 1920s. During a landmark walk with oral historian Eric Mischnick, Emil felt this pull (although he never acknowledged it) to reinforce the hardships throughout his stories of fun and enjoyment. Emil, for instance, reminisced about hunting gophers year-round, but then took care to mention that his father kept the money on occasion, or that he received no allowance as a child. These side notes reinforced his ethnic group's collective memory of hardship, yet his individual memories reveal another part to this story: Emil

---

[40]Clark, "Germans from Russia on the Northern Plains," 198–232.

[41]For more information on the complexities of the new German-Russian story, see "'*We didn't know any better*': Growing up German Russian" in Clark, "Germans from Russia on the Northern Plains," 303–16.

had fun as a child. He recounted a time when he and his brother had their older brother take the gopher tails into Napoleon, North Dakota. This, they hoped, ensured that they would receive the money. And they did. They took the money and bought a .22 single-shot rifle. They were able, Emil remembered, to order ammunition from Sears, Roebuck, and Company for about fifteen cents a box. Having this new rifle increased their gopher tails production, Emil said. With a rifle and a shot gun, they always had someone to follow up the shot if the first person missed. "We shot at everything," Emil says. They may have had to work to earn their money in those days, but as Emil revealed, they had fun doing it.[42]

---

[42]Emil Roesler, interview by Eric Mischnick, June 8, 2008, DVD, Dakota Memories.

Great Depression Buildings and the Social Value of Work in German-Russian Country

by Steve C. Martens[1]

[1]Steve C. Martens retired as Professor Emeritus in Architecture at North Dakota State University and is past President of the North Dakota State Historical Board. He has worked as a historical architect and research historian specializing in historic context studies, National Register nominations, heritage landscapes and vernacular material culture, HABS/HAER/MHPR recordation, preservation planning, historic building assessment studies, local design guidelines, adaptive use design, and rehabilitation of historic architecture.

Old buildings can tell many stories if we listen to them in the right way. In this case, the story is of the Great Depression and Dust Bowl survival on the northern plains. A series of field trips sponsored by the grassroots organization Preservation North Dakota in 2012 afforded a stimulating opportunity to revisit the rich heritage of Depression era buildings in German-Russian Country. Depression buildings and landscapes tell a story about the importance of work in sustaining communities on the northern Great Plains. The poignant story of Dust Bowl survival and federal work relief programs are reflected in buildings constructed in North Dakota's "Sauerkraut Triangle," at the core of German-Russian settlement.[2] Nearly everyone in America suffered during the Depression years, but on the harsh northern Great Plains the experiences of recent-immigrant groups like the German-Russians was different in several respects.

Regional scholars have considered North Dakota's Depression landscapes and architectural heritage from a variety of perspectives.[3] By appreciating the assortment of pragmatically beautiful buildings with our own eyes, useful lessons about cultural values can still be discovered some seventy years after they were built. Based on a 2010 statewide research project sponsored by the State Historical Society of North Dakota, the rich variety of Depression work relief buildings in southcentral North Dakota is revealed.[4] Buildings can best be understood in terms

[2]Father William Sherman's endearing term, also referred to by others as "the Great Sauerkraut Pyramid."

[3]Gordon L. Iseminger, Elwyn Robinson, William Sherman, Lorena Hickok, Jerome Tweton, Daniel Rylance, and Ted Jelliff have each authored helpful frameworks for appreciating the kinds of buildings and landscapes architectural historians refer to as "material culture."

[4]Steve C. Martens, "Federal Relief Construction in North Dakota, 1931–1943," National Register of Historic Places for the U.S. Department of the Interior, October 2011, http://history.nd.gov/hp/PDFinfo/MPDF%20Complete%20Rev%2010_2010.pdf.

of their history and cultural significance, in this case focusing on the local story of promotion, pride, and renewal. Buildings embody the history and memory of North Dakota German-Russian culture during the Great Depression. It is a meaningful history and a fascinating memory well worth revisiting in appreciation of how different our lives today are, and the extent to which those lasting cultural values of investment, effort, and spiritual renewal can still underpin our communities nearly a century later. The underlying lessons in the durable legacy of regionally distinctive buildings have much to do with their embodiment of community and productive work as essential human values. Buildings helped restore a spirit of hopefulness, worth, and renewal.

Buildings also tell us about patterns of historical events. Examine the evidence with your own eyes. At a crisis time, federal agencies responded to exhausted lands and exhausted people. Useful and sustainable building projects, like the finely hand-crafted Wishek Civic Auditorium, had much to do with the embodiment of productive work as an essential human value. The principle of stewardship toward architectural heritage is one of the most important investments a community can make in environmental sustainability and spiritual renewal that respects these gifts from the past. Practical and beautiful buildings like the Wishek Auditorium were gifts made seventy-five years ago by McIntosh County residents. This fieldstone building with long span laminated wood arches is a masterpiece of design and construction effort, acknowledged and told in informative detail on the City of Wishek web page link.[5] One of the important, durable values we can associate with the heritage of German-Russians is that when they build or improve something, they intend to make it last, which includes an unending responsibility to care for the upkeep and maintenance.

[5]"Wishek Civic Center," internet link maintained by the City of Wishek, ND, http://www.wishek-nd.com/cityinfo/civic-center.html.

Wishek Civic Auditorium WPA project in German-Russian Country, employing picturesque rustic fieldstone design by Jamestown architect Gilbert R. Horton. *Note: Unless indicated otherwise, images for this chapter are by Steve C. Martens and used with his permission.*

Talking about the Great Depression and Dust Bowl can become very depressing if we focus on the sacrifices and disappointments and failures people experienced through no fault of their own. In a moment I'm going to need to give a bit more detail about some of the local conditions during the "Dirty Thirties." But a great deal of good came out of the investments of human spirit, energy, creative thinking, and extraordinarily hard work. Analysis can focus attention on some of those positive aspects of local culture here in the German-Russian Country, especially things we can still see on the landscape that were built or made under those dire circumstances. Thus, the buildings and landscapes created by German-Russians under New Deal sponsorship reflect a necessary cultural negotiation between the notions of charity and an honest exchange of relief work for pay. Buildings like the beautifully cared-for Wishek Auditorium, with its granite fieldstones and hand-built arches, can teach us much about values, priorities, sustainability, and most of all, about the importance of work in sustaining life.

From the standpoint of architectural history, buildings and landscapes from the Depression era are distinctive in several respects. Although regional in their materials and character, the New Deal buildings in German-Russian Country reveal a discontinuity and a break from a distinct cultural tradition of building forms and functionality imported by immigrant German-Russians. Rather, the buildings reflect a kind of homogenization of design under emerging national trends. Guided by academically trained architects and emergent national tastes for Art Deco and picturesque rustic styles, these buildings are part of an architectural tradition born out of austerity and commitment to do without, but with reluctant willingness to accept external support that led to continuing assimilation of German-Russian communities into the national culture. The architectural styles and palette of materials are not very typical of buildings being built today, so we notice those differences first. But the more compelling story has more to do with what the buildings and the work they entailed meant to local people who constructed them.

Economic, social, and environmental conditions in North Dakota in 1931 impacted an entire region and fundamentally changed the lives of an entire generation of hard-working immigrant families. In *The Dust Bowl*, documentary film director Ken Burns demonstrates the extent to which the environmental disaster compounded unemployment and economic collapse and broke the spirit of many North Dakotans who were already well accustomed to suffering and deprivation. Without belaboring the point, for about eight years things in North Dakota were about as bad as they could possibly get. Historian Gordon L. Iseminger interpreted those same circumstances insightfully based on his analysis of oral interviews recorded from North Dakotans during the 1930s and shortly thereafter. One article in particular, published in *North Dakota History: Journal of the Northern Plains* in 1984 and reproduced online through the Germans from Russia Society internet link, focuses particular detail on conditions in McIntosh County, based on firsthand oral history recordings in the collections of the University of North Dakota library. Excerpting from Dr. Iseminger's article:

> Most German-Russians were poor when they arrived in McIntosh County, but they were young and they had hope. Accustomed to suffering and adversity, they worked hard, they took up land under the Homestead and Pre-emption Acts, and they prospered. During the 1930s, however, many were again poor, they had lost their youth, and hope was waning. The Depression seemed endless. Even the elements were against them. The temperature extremes and the droughts that German-Russians had experienced while on the Russian steppes and while pioneering on the Dakota plains were nothing compared to those they experienced during the 1930s. McIntosh County, where farming was the industry on which the social and economic welfare of the people depended, was cited by the Works Progress Administration as an area of intense drought distress for the years 1930–36.
>
> There was less moisture in the soil in McIntosh County at the beginning of 1935 than at any time since statehood had been granted in 1889. People despaired of its ever snowing or raining again, and farmers were hesitant to prepare fields for spring seeding. Crop prospects were dimmed, unfortunately, in mid-July by high temperatures, rust, and army worms. Much small grain was not worth harvesting; not even the straw had any feed value. By the end

> of the summer, cattle were dying of thirst and starvation. Farmers had no money with which to purchase seed grain for 1935. Also in 1935, *encephalomyelitis*, an infectious brain disease affecting horses, spread rapidly through the county. Many farmers could afford neither the serum nor the services of a veterinarian and were losing their horses just when they were most needed for field work.[6]

Efforts to manage the crisis locally and at the state level by populist governor William Langer may have been noble, but the problem was much too great to be remediated locally. The urgent need for an emergency program of federal relief in the Great Plains states was evident at the beginning of Franklin Delano Roosevelt's first term as president. Roosevelt dispatched Lorena Hickok, a skilled newspaperwoman, to essentially be the eyes, ears and conscience of his administration on the ground. In 1933, Harry Hopkins assigned Hickok, "to go around the country and look this thing over. I don't want statistics from you. I don't want the social worker angle. I just want your own reaction as an ordinary citizen [to the effectiveness of the work relief programs in assisting destitute victims of the Great Depression on the northern Plains]."[7] Throughout 1933 and 1934, Lorena Hickok traveled the length and breadth of the Great Plains, reporting directly to Hopkins, FDR, and Eleanor Roosevelt. In North Dakota, she concluded, a majority of farmers and ranchers were irredeemably bankrupt. Conditions in North Dakota were about as bad—probably worse—than in any state in the US at that time, she reported, noting:

---

[6]All excerpted from Gordon L. Iseminger, in *North Dakota History: Journal of the Northern Plains 51, no.3* (Summer 1984): 4–23; reproduced under the title, "The McIntosh County German-Russians: The First Fifty Years," accessed from the GHRC web link at http://library.ndsu.edu/grhc/articles/magazines/articles/mcintosh.html.

[7]Richard Lowitt, 1984, 8. See also Lorena Hickok's original reports from the field in Lowitt and Beasley, eds., *One Third of a Nation: Lorena Hickok Reports on the Great Depression* (2000).

> Their houses had gone to ruins. No Repairs for years. Their furniture, dishes, cooking utensils—no replacement in years. No bed linen, and quilts and blankets had all gone. A year ago their clothing was rags. This year they hardly have rags.[8]

Nowhere in her travels on the Great Plains did Hickok see, learn, or report anything that exceeded the misery—the destitution—she found in North Dakota, although conditions in South Dakota reportedly came close.[9] There is strong indication of FDR's special commitment to North Dakota and the Great Plains throughout his three terms in office, evinced by the range and scope of federal construction projects undertaken in the state, the persistence of planning efforts to ameliorate a distressed landscape, and in terms of promotional documentation, publicity, and recurrent visits to the state by FDR and his senior advisors.

Though its presentation was hyperbolic, Pare Lorentz's 1936 documentary film *The Plow That Broke the Plains* drew several correlations between technology of World War I and the introduction of destructive technology to agricultural practices on the Great Plains, reflecting a fundamental change in the rural American way of life.[10] This crisis threatened the very fabric of society.[11] Federal and state governments began to confront the perceived possibility of a Soviet Bolshevist type of social and political insurrection, and abandonment of the failed capitalist economic model (bearing in mind that the Russian revolutionary example was, at the time, a scant fifteen years old).[12] On a weekly basis, newspa-

---

[8]Quoted here exactly as punctuation and capitalization appear in the original text of Hickok's reports.
[9]Richard Lowitt, The New Deal and the West (Bloomington: Indiana University Press, 1984), 8–14.
[10]Pare Lorentz. *The Plow That Broke the Plains* (documentary film), US Resettlement Administration, 1936. The film is currently distributed in a variety of readily accessible formats, including digital on-line versions.
[11]Arthur M. Schlesinger, Jr., *The Coming of the New Deal, 1933–1935: The Age of Roosevelt*, (Boston: Mariner Books, 2003), 275.
[12]Anthony J. Badger, *New Deal: The Depression Years, 1933–1940* (Chicago: Ivan R. Dee, 2002), 38–41.

pers from the mid-1930s are full of sensational heart-wrenching stories about families being decimated and of gruesome murder-suicides where families simply could no longer cope.

The combined consequences of drought, poor crops, and depressed farm prices were soon apparent. There was an uncharacteristic air of wistfulness about the children. Christian Klipfel, who farmed fifteen miles east of Ashley, was driven by financial worries and despondency to take his own life on January 27, 1934. The number of those owning their farms declined between 1930–1935, and farm tenancy increased from 284 in 1930 to 334 in 1935. Tenancy had once been a steppingstone to farm ownership, but now it was an indication that older farmers were unable to become or remain owners.[13]

North Dakotans experienced real trauma in the 1930s, probably beyond our ability to comprehend. Because drought added to the difficulties caused by the Depression, North Dakota suffered more than much of the rest of the nation.[14] From 1935 to 1940, some 86,000 persons fled North Dakota for the proverbial "greener pastures."[15] Of all the cultures that inhabited the Great Plains, perhaps the German-Russians had prepared themselves best—to suffer deprivation, environmental and economic collapse—of all the groups of immigrant farmers. The first generation of German-Russian immigrants and the generation that preceded them on the steppes of Ukraine and South Russia had mastered many skills and much tolerance for doing without. But even from the perspective of seventy-five-years' distance, it seems there should be a limit on the human suffering and the toll the Great Depression caused to families and communities.

The Depression years were bad everywhere, but the circumstances of sustaining a life of subsistence agriculture on the northern plains through the Dust Bowl years made the expe-

---

[13]Iseminger, quoting *Ashley Tribune*, April 12, 1933, February 1, 1934.

[14]Elwyn B. Robinson, *History of North Dakota* (Lincoln: University of Nebraska Press, 1966), 396–97, 419.

[15]Robinson, *History of North Dakota*, 1–16.

rience of the German-Russians especially difficult. Near Mott, the John Stern family members recounted events from the era of the Great Depression, when transient hobos riding the rails were welcomed to the Stern home for a handout of food, a gesture of kindness and generosity from an immigrant family whose own resources must clearly have been stretched. John Stern talked openly about the early hard times in a 1957 *Mott Pioneer Press* interview.[16] He said they could tell changes in the weather by the way the coyotes howled on the prairie. In one instance, the family had to kill newborn calves because there wasn't enough feed for extra animals. The Stern's son Reinhold left the farm in the late '30s and joined the Civilian Conservation Corps for two years. He was stationed in Fargo with about three hundred other young men. His salary was thirty dollars per month, and all except five dollars was sent back home to his parents.

Previously, periods of recession and indigence were relieved at the local level with "home relief," usually in the form of food or heating assistance. Occasionally, some communities provided labor-intensive "made" work in order for the able-bodied poor to prove their willingness to work.[17] Local efforts to ameliorate poverty depended heavily on charity, unfortunately reflecting the conventional attitude of the day (also held by the Hoover administration) that anyone genuinely willing to work could find a job. With an estimated seven million unemployed in 1930 increasing to fourteen million in 1933, it became obvious that willingness to work alone would not yield a job. A new approach was needed to meet the joblessness and declining spirits of the nation. Faltering local economies and earlier problems administering work relief at the state level made it imperative for the federal government to actively engage in a relief solution.

---

[16]The Stern family's experience during the Depression was recounted in a National Register of Historic Places nomination for the family's traditional stone home and connected livestock barn that has been preserved near Mott as part of the legacy of first-generation German-Russians.
[17]Federal Works Agency.

But there were particular difficulties with getting participation in relief programs from North Dakotans, and especially proud German-Russians, who appeared prepared to starve on the farm rather than accept charity. The exchange of labor for relief payments suggested an alternative recourse:

> The willingness of the German-Russians of McIntosh County to accept government assistance was not an admission of failure or an indication that after fifty years in America they had lost their determination and self-reliance. It was an admission that under the circumstances they could not help themselves. Government programs were their only recourse, but they did not want something for nothing. According to H. D. Piper, head of the local Federal Emergency Relief Office, McIntosh County led the state in "work off relief." By the end of April 1935, McIntosh County recipients had worked off 97.4 percent of the relief contracted under the Federal Emergency Relief Administration. The figure for most counties was between 30 and 40 percent. McIntosh County residents appreciated the help they received and insisted on giving labor in return.[18]

Most of all, there was an awareness of the pressing and imminent need to *do something* to change the economic circumstances and the general malaise. Faltering local economies and earlier problems administering work relief at the state level made it imperative for the federal government to actively engage in a relief solution. Roosevelt's New Deal advocated work relief to replace the "dole." Concepts of "direct relief" and "useful public work" tended to shift supervision of relief projects away from local, independent contractors and toward a state agency of the federal government as the "employer of last resort." Speaking of the purposes of the WPA, Roosevelt's "minister of relief," Harry Hopkins, stated the new administration's most basic premise:

---

[18]Iseminger, quoting *Ashley Tribune*, June 13, 1935.

> Work relief costs more than direct relief, but the cost is justified. First, in the saving of morale. Second, in the preservation of human skills and talents. Third, in the material enrichment which the unemployed add to our national wealth through their labors.[19]

Roosevelt's New Deal vigorously advocated work relief to replace the dole. The Roosevelt administration initiated a flurry of legislation to provide jobs and inject dollars into the depressed economy, coordinated by Harry Hopkins, whose remarkably coherent personal vision influenced the direction of all subsequent work relief programs. A farm boy from Iowa, Hopkins spoke with passion:

> Look at these fields, these forests and rivers. America is the richest country in the world. We can afford to pay for anything we want. And we want a decent life for all the people in this country. And we are going to pay for it.[20]

The New Deal federal work relief programs are an "alphabet soup" of acronyms.[21] The Federal Emergency Relief Administration (FERA), the Civilian Conservation Corps (CCC), the Agricultural Adjustment Act (AAA), the National Industrial Recovery Act (NIRA), and the Public Works Administration (PWA) were among the first of these programs, already in place by the end of the first Hundred Days. Among other activities, FERA trained social workers, it mixed grasshopper bait, it organized recreational programs; and it sponsored the arts and historical research. At the peak of its emergency work relief program during the winter of 1933–34,

---

[19]Searle F. Charles, *Minister of Relief: Harry Hopkins and the Great Depression* (Syracuse, NY: Syracuse University Press, 1963).

[20]Charles, *Minister of Relief.* This revealing quote appears in *Minister of Relief* and has recently been reintroduced by June Hopkins in an article, "The Road Not Taken: Harry Hopkins and New Deal Work Relief," in *Presidential Studies Quarterly* 29, no. 2 (June 1999).

[21]The conveniently understandable catch phrase "alphabet soup" has been summarily applied to analysis of these myriad federal agencies from the very beginning. See, for example, Adam Cohen (2009), 274.

Emmons County Courthouse in Linton was a typical PWA project in German-Russian Country, employing Art Deco architectural design by Minot architects Bugenhagen, Deeter, and Hess.

the Civil Works Administration (CWA) employed about thirty-seven thousand persons in North Dakota. The Public Works Administration (or PWA, and of course the similar-sounding acronyms start to get confusing here) assisted with larger, harder-to-construct buildings like the Emmons County Courthouse in Linton, and Streeter school. These projects were typically constructed by established building contractors, rather than by pieced together workforces of laborers. But the greatest impacts on North Dakota's renewal came from two programs; the CCC and the WPA.[22]

[22]Several of the federal work relief initiatives were led by notable North Dakotans who figured in programs nationally. Among them: Thomas F. Moodie, Judge A.M. Christianson, Bertha Rachel Palmer, Russell Reid, Joseph Stoeckler, and J. Clark Salyers. The Honorable James Francis T. O'Connor is commemorated with a granite monument in Grand Forks inscribed with the accolade, (attributed to President Franklin Delano Roosevelt), "Comptroller of the Currency of the United States, 1933–1938. He kept the banks sound and your money safe."

Depression era federal work-relief building projects were a coordinated, designed response to a context that had emerged over the preceding forty years. In the 1930s, each program identified the rules and objectives that would guide its implementation. The various relief programs reflect several distinct public policy objectives. Perhaps most fundamental was the impact of exchanging work for pay as opposed to direct payments or charity to the unemployed. In the end, FDR's vision was more palatable to the public and more effectual in altering the landscape of destitution.

German-Russians characteristically required very little to satisfy their needs, and they traditionally withstood hard times without asking for help from the government. They looked after themselves, they helped each other, and they went without. During the 1930s, however, McIntosh County German-Russians accepted, and sometimes demanded, emergency relief. There were never enough funds to hire all of the young people who wanted to enroll in the Civilian Conservation Corps and the National Youth Administration, and McIntosh County officials bid eagerly for participation in the federal Prairie States Forestry, or shelterbelt, Project. At a mass meeting held in Ashley on November 30, 1936, resolutions were passed and sent to North Dakota's congressmen calling for a special session of Congress if necessary in order that WPA employment for both farmers and urban workers could be continued.[23]

Relief era programs went beyond creating jobs to create social structures that enfranchised a much broader segment of the public. The first, explicit policy objective was to create employment and to get wage earners to spend money in the local economy. Though this chapter is written from the viewpoint of an architectural historian (someone interested in learning from old buildings), some of the most touching accounts are about people who contributed their labor through the WPA and other work relief programs that included garden tomatoes canned by farm

[23]Iseminger, quoting *Wishek News*, August 13, 1936.

women for distribution through commodity food programs, home canning projects, and the numbers of blankets and coats sewn in work relief sewing rooms. Those programs, too, reinforced the point of doing tangible work that benefited others, in exchange for modest income payments.

Some of the earliest New Deal construction projects authorized by FDR from 1934–1936 were undertaken by FERA and the Civil Works Administration (CWA), using traditional building construction contracting methods for large-scale projects like county courthouses. Similarly, the PWA tended toward larger-scale projects including town schools like the ones in Streeter, Ashley, and Edgeley. The principal relief program relevant to building construction, the Works Progress Administration (WPA), also began under Hopkins's direction. As a federal work relief program, the WPA intended to provide 3.5 million jobs almost immediately. The WPA's mandate had a number of specific provisions relevant to buildings like the Hague Fire Hall and City Office constructed under WPA auspices and local sponsorship. Among the guidelines:

> A. Projects should be useful, with a local sponsor.
> B. There should be considerable expenditure for labor as opposed to materials.
> C. Projects should be planned and reviewed so that expenditures for labor could be immediate.
> D. Preference should be given to persons on relief roles (many unskilled workers).
> E. Projects were to be allocated to geographic areas with the greatest number of persons on relief rolls.
> F. Projects should put the maximum number of people to work in a short time, while allowing reasonable opportunities for private employment.[24]

[24]Paraphrasing from *WPA Circular*; June 15, 1935. The provision that projects should provide considerable return to the federal Treasury has been omitted from this list as not relevant to the discussion.

There was some latent reluctance for communities to get involved with these projects. But with vigorous encouragement from Hopkins's office, applications were promptly prepared and submitted by the state emergency relief office. The WPA work-relief programs, in particular, encouraged investment in small, ambitious, readily achievable projects that were envisioned by local communities. With almost all WPA projects originated, sponsored, and designed at the local or state level, the likelihood that a particular project would be realized was largely dependent upon efforts of local individuals. The application process was streamlined in such a way that whatever a local sponsor asked for, they were almost certain to be awarded funds for labor to accomplish it. District offices exerted little or no review or comment regarding locally sponsored designs, particularly for projects under the suggested $25,000 limit. The federal government remained more concerned about the employment opportunities afforded by each project, than the scope or even utility of the project. Farm-to-market roads were improved and virtually every small community in the state still has a ball field, tennis court, or hockey rink built by WPA work relief labor. As reported by Robinson in *History of North Dakota*,

> In North Dakota . . . the WPA alone . . . built 20,373 miles of highways and streets, 721 new bridges, 166 miles of sidewalks, 15,012 culverts, 503 new public buildings, 61 additions to public buildings, 680 outdoor recreation facilities . . . 809 water wells, 2 irrigation projects, 39 sewage treatment plants, and 9 water treatment plants. It reconstructed 1,002 bridges and viaducts, 2,180 public buildings and 1,721 culverts. It repaired 646,206 books, served 3,653,392 school lunches, and sewed 2,078,451 garments.[25]

[25]Summary statistics for each of the main work relief programs were tabulated by Robinson, *History of North Dakota*, 408. It is noteworthy that each work relief program kept a detailed accounting of the completed projects, which benefitted the public relations promotion of these federally funded projects.

In terms of their planning, the work relief projects reveal a more scientific approach to buildings and civic institutions that is reflected in schools, healthcare, public institutions, wildlife habitat, and management of scarce water resources. The period of the 1930s was the first serious attempt at modifying the landscape based on scientific methods of analysis. Depression era water management projects and soil conservation projects (like the two CCC camps near Wishek) rehabilitated landscapes, constructed shelterbelts, and did grasshopper abatement. Intervention strategies focused on water resource management and mitigation of environmental degradation. Ultimately, it may be shown that the greatest impact of relief work was in renewing the spirit of hopefulness and worth on the part of the public, especially in small towns and the rural countryside. In all these instances, the spiritual value of work and the ability to improve a bad situation by reasoned and coordinated interventions were among the lasting impacts of the federal relief work.

Depression era New Deal work relief programs had lasting impacts we can see in North Dakota communities and on the rural landscape today. Summary statistics help to tell the story, but not as well as the buildings themselves. Consider the range of building types and architectural treatments in towns and on the North Dakota landscape. Note the wide variety of project scales based on identifiable need in communities of varying sizes. The work relief construction projects reflect architectural styles that were popular under the New Deal work relief programs. The work relief building projects were architecturally innovative in the 1930s, and they still stand out distinctively on the landscape today. Streamlined Art Deco/*Moderne* styles prevailed in buildings like the Venturia Village Hall and Lehr City Hall. They contrast markedly with picturesque rustic fieldstone buildings like the Wishek Auditorium and Bathhouse. Work was focused specifically on programs that offered immediate relief income payments in exchange for work to complete constructed projects that served the public good (broadly defined). These were ambitious building projects that applied a sophisticated, scientific approach to the design of public buildings like courthouses, schools, and even infrastructure improvements to rehabilitate a degraded natural landscape.

From a historical perspective, the tangible legacy of the New Deal era can be observed in the constructed projects nationwide and especially within the state of North Dakota. I believe we can find an abundance of evidence that it was the works projects that restored worker confidence, put food on the table, ameliorated the myriad consequences of economic collapse, and produced much of the infrastructure we continue to use today. The construction projects are distinctive as symbols of the variety of federal interventions, accomplished by laborious work relief effort, embodying investment in community and spiritual renewal for

Venturia City Offices and WPA Auditorium (often referred to locally as The Armory), an impressive small-scale example of site cast concrete WPA Art Deco architecture near the South Dakota border.

workers and their communities alike. Rural communities were validated. The underlying story is in the tangible difference these programs made on people's lives, and the way our future as a society was envisioned.

Functionally sophisticated and architecturally innovative county courthouses were built in German-Russian Country, like Emmons County Courthouse in Linton, Sheridan County Courthouse in McCluskey, and Hettinger County Courthouse in Mott. These buildings reflect a significant upgrade in delivery of county governmental services and as county judicial centers. Art Deco details and geometric architectural motifs reveal architectural tastes introduced from outside sources and appear unexpected-

Lehr City Hall and Fire Station (WPA) in the contrasting Art Deco architectural style (unattributed).

WPA picturesque rustic bath house in Wishek; a surviving remnant of the federal investment in recreational infrastructure for small communities on the Great Plains, and still serviceable seventy years later.

ly in small buildings for municipal government like Hague Fire Hall, Lehr City Hall, and Venturia City Hall/Auditorium (referred to locally as The Armory). Other notable places for civic assembly and recreational use, including the Zeeland Auditorium, New England Veterans Memorial Building, and Glen Ullin Civic Auditorium, remain in active use today. Also notable for the same, innovative Art Deco architectural motifs are the Mandan and Devils Lake War Memorial buildings in more urban parts of the state. Ambitious Art Deco school designs were used in Williston, Dickinson, Bismarck, and Devils Lake. The Streeter School in the southwest corner of Stutsman County is the last Art Deco survivor from a set of three similar town schools constructed by the PWA from 1933 to 1937.[26] Other smaller and more modest

[26]The three schools and other civic investments by the PWA were proudly affirmed with a graphic map in a June 22, 1937, article in the *Grand Forks Herald*: "PWA Cites Results After Four Years of Activities in North Dakota."

Hettinger County Courthouse in Mott (1936) was a typical CWA project in German-Russian Country, employing Art Deco design by Minot architects Bugenhagen, Hess, and Deeter. Though modest in its Art Deco details, among local residents the design is sometimes compared in its architectural aspirations with the North Dakota State Capitol.

designs for ideal model rural schools were proposed to the State School Superintendent as an a la carte set by North Dakota architects like Gilbert Horton and Arthur Van Horn.[27]

Equally important community buildings and civic auditoriums were constructed in Medina, Robinson, Steele, and Wishek, all in the stylistically contrasting fieldstone picturesque rustic style (sometimes referred to as WPA Rustic). Fieldstone rustic buildings for recreation and tourism were promoted by Ethel Schlasinger's 1938 *WPA Writers' Guide to North Dakota*. In counties with concentrations of German-Russians, they included

[27]Barbara Beving Long, Mss5469 and Mss5470, 1991, in the collections of the State Historical Society of North Dakota.

Hague Fire Hall and City Offices. The WPA design is attributed to Bismarck architects Van Horn and Ritterbush.

Zeeland Hall (1938) WPA in the less common American Colonial Revival architectural style.

Art Deco influenced Streeter Public School, the last survivor of three innovative and modern schools constructed in southcentral North Dakota by the PWA in 1936. The other two schools were in Ashley and Edgeley.

Wishek Pool Bathhouse, Zeeland City Park, Crystal Springs Fountain, and other local tourist parks and camps. Guided by the vision and imagination of State Historical Society Director Russell Reid, state parks and historic sites were developed under CCC and WPA work relief sponsorship including the Whitestone Hill Battlefield picnic shelter and Fort Abraham Lincoln south of Mandan, which continues to interpret its CCC legacy through the beautifully preserved fieldstone park museum building, appropriately dedicated to the CCC work crews.

The relief work projects are distinctive in terms of their architectural style, materials, and manner of construction. They also addressed historic events and circumstances that had social, political, economic, and environmental dimensions. The professions of architecture, engineering, landscape architecture, planning, and construction were largely transformed by the manner in which they implemented work relief projects through design and construction. Much of the architectural, engineering,

Medina Auditorium and City Offices. WPA picturesque rustic architecture by Gilbert R. Horton.

Steele City Hall, Civic Auditorium, and Fire Hall with WPA fieldstone attributed to Jamestown architect Gilbert R. Horton.

Fieldstone entrance gate to the Zeeland City Park and tourist camp.

Whitestone Hill State Park picnic shelter, faithfully reconstructed in 2011 to honor the original WPA design following a tragic arson fire. A great many North Dakota state parks and historic sites were developed by CCC and WPA crews under the vision of Historical Society Superintendent Russell Reid.

and construction legacy of the Depression era continues to be utilized as a set of valuable public assets more than seventy years after the relief programs ended. In a rural, agriculturally dependent state like North Dakota, direct relief programs provided necessary short-term relief from destitution for many individual families. Perhaps useful correlations can be drawn with respect to the multi-faceted role of federal government, benefits of public investment in constructed infrastructure, and the affirmative social value associated with productive work as a fundamental human need.

The important achievements of North Dakota CCC crews are interpreted at Fort Abraham Lincoln State Part south of Mandan, the intake site from which North Dakota CCC companies were established.

Some of the interesting work relief construction projects in central North Dakota call attention to something that was new to the nation in the 1920s and 30s; that is, they served the public purpose of promoting recreational tourism and broad public learning about the state. The supporting rationale for state historic sites and environmental rehabilitation activities of the 1930s is well-substantiated in period literature, like the *WPA Writers' Guide to North Dakota: The Northern Prairie State.* In perhaps North Dakota's first ever endeavor into ecotourism, the WPA Writers Guide promulgated a series of recommended tours that encouraged the public to discover North Dakota, including fascinating features like the Zeeland City Park entrance gate. The federal *Writers' Guide* invited people to become familiar with North Dakota through tours like the Crystal Springs wayside fountain and several tourist parks along US12, US10, and US2. Of potential further interest to readers who may wish to visit these fascinating buildings, a sampler of images of North Dakota's work relief building projects are featured prominently in the book *Buildings of North Dakota.*[28]

Crystal Springs is an especially good example of work relief geared toward tourism, for which we have fairly complete historical documentation. With growing importance of Highway 10 to the traveling public, wayside stops at convenient distances were an important amenity to the traveling public. Early automobiles required frequent replenishment of both motor oil and radiator coolant water. Though it is small and currently neglected, the historic Crystal Springs wayside fountain has National Register significance for importance to the popularity of automobile travel along US Highway 10 and for its association with historic events of the Depression era. The fountain represents a modest but significant contribution to the local community by providing an attractive amenity, recreational activities, or community services, which wcrc prcviously unavailablc. Thc fountain was constructed with thoughtfully crafted indigenous materials, reflecting a distinctive construction method.

Arthur H. Geisler, a local farmer and itinerant stoneworker from Crystal Springs, was one of the builders of the wayside fountain.[29] As the farm son of German-American immigrant parents in the 1920s and 30s, it was still common for German-American children (boys in particular) to leave school after eighth grade to help with farming, and that appears to be the case for Arthur. Anecdotal information suggests that Arthur may have been exposed to stone construction work through family ties to another family of Geislers (or Geiszlers) from the Kulm area. This

---

[28]Steve Martens and Ron Ramsay, *Buildings of North Dakota* (Charlotte: University of Virginia Press, 2015). Excerpts also accessible at https://sah-archipedia.org/.

[29]See Martens 2010 MPDF study for more on Geisler (b. 31 March 1911; d. 6 April 1990).

Family photo taken at historic Crystal Springs roadside fountain. *Image courtesy of the private collections of Marlys White, Steele, North Dakota.*

was probably the same Geiszler family that worked with Gilbert Horton to demonstrate stone cutting techniques for the Medina Auditorium. Constructing the stone fountain was sponsored by the North Dakota State Highway Department under a statewide Works Progress Administration grant for a number of small wayside improvements statewide. The opportunity to obtain about four months of work hauling stones and building the fountain brought important resources to families of the young men who built the wayside fountain at a wage rate of $10.40 per week.

In April 1934, 148,000 people, or more than one-fifth of North Dakota's population, were receiving financial assistance from the federal government, either direct relief or some form of work relief. By the time FERA was discontinued in 1935, the agency had built 114 dams, 3 municipal wells, 60 bridges, 986 sanitary privies, 70 public buildings, 14 swimming pools, and 23 parks.[30] Though the economic malaise continued for more than a decade, these boldly interventionist programs provided a turning point from which the Roosevelt's New Deal team was able to address the worst economic crisis in America's history. While many of the initial New Deal programs provided direct relief to people in dire economic need, the emerging programs fueled the economy with employment opportunities that resulted in construction of historically significant buildings, sites, and water resource management structures statewide in North Dakota, but the basic objective was to restore purchasing power to bolster a flatlined national income. This program elicited immediate support from construction periodicals, such as the regional publication *The Improvement Bulletin*, which proclaimed, "A nationally launched construction program will supply employment to idle men and restore purchasing power, and will hasten the day of emergence from the depression cycle."[31]

Rocks for the Medina City Hall building were gathered from a twenty-mile radius. Forty-five men were employed to split and

[30] Robinson, 406.

[31] *Construction Bulletin*. Minneapolis, MN weekly; (May 19, 1933): 1-2.

shape the rocks. Late in his life, architect Gilbert R. Horton, Fellow of the American Institute of Architects, spoke proudly of working with local stonemasons to teach laborers the methods of splitting those rocks. In 1972 he told the *Jamestown Sun*, "Watching those boys learn to select the right rock for the right place was a real thrill. The walls, they're just as sound today as the day they were put in place."[32] Rocks cropped up with frost action most everywhere in glaciated North Dakota, and Horton combined available labor with the indigenous material to construct lasting buildings that reflect pride in community. Of course, Horton wasn't the only architect working in this milieu. The Medina City Hall exhibits exceptionally well crafted randomly coursed ashlar stonework. It was built relatively late during the Depression, toward the end of federal work relief projects.

Several firsthand accounts have been shared about job-site working conditions on projects like this one. One of the best is the version retold on the Wishek Auditorium internet page. Sixty men generally worked eight- to ten-hour days. The rock was sorted by color and size, and crews were assigned to prepare it for placement. According to one of the rock finishers, Dan Rudolph, the foreman would mark the wall with the size and color rock needed. A two-man team consisting of a rock finisher and a helper would sign their name to the area marked, then begin squaring a rock to fit the space. The finisher held a large chisel, while the helper hit it with a sledgehammer. After the rock was squared the helper hauled away the waste pieces while the finisher shaped the front of the rock with a small chisel and hammer. If the rock had any chisel marks or broken corners it was discarded and the team would start over. It could take a couple of hours, or several days, to finish a rock depending on one's luck with the chisel and quality of the rock. After the rocks were shaped, another crew would cement them in place.[33]

---

[32]Long, interview in the *Jamestown Sun*, quoted by Long in "The Evolution of Gilbert R. Horton, Architects," manuscript in the collections of the State Historical Society of North Dakota, 1991:11–12.
[33]"Wishek Civic Center," internet link maintained by the City of Wishek, ND, https://wishek-nd.com/all-about-wishek/german-russian-heritage/

Long span Fargo Arena under construction by WPA crews in 1936, according to an Art Moderne design by Fargo architect S. Marius Houkom. *Image provided courtesy of the Institute for Regional Studies, North Dakota State University Archives.*

Another illustrative account comes to us from the experience of Fargo architect Marius Houkom. In 1937, Houkom designed the Island Park swimming pool, a Works Progress Administration project, mainly to put unemployed carpenters to work. Houkom said he was trained in college to design buildings efficiently and economically, using technologically advanced materials. But the Island Park pool and Fargo Ice Arena presented unique challenges for a young architect just out of school. "Along comes the Depression, and [Houkom] said he had to develop a new criteria for design. The criteria wasn't to build cheaply or efficiently, the criteria was to put people to work."[34] The result was buildings

[34]Steven P. Wagner, "Designs Stand the Test of Time," *Fargo Forum*, December 12, 1999, quoting an interview between architectural historian Ron Ramsey and Fargo architect S. Marius Houkom.

constructed from a hybrid of local materials, and the revival of some antiquated handwork methods of construction.

Generally speaking, stoneworking was accomplished at the project site under the supervision of a master mason directing the activities of crews of semi-skilled stonecutters. On average, one hour's labor was required to finish each stone.[35] Because jobsite safety was a priority consideration of the WPA, workers were outfitted with protective eyewear and stonecutting proceeded in small beehive-shaped enclosures. According to the WPA's literature of the time, the purpose of such safety programs was meant to be "more instructional than administrative."[36] Regarding one rural school project near Fargo, the *Fargo Forum* wrote:

> The architects themselves gave lessons in cutting and dressing the stone, studying the boulders to find the grain, illustrating how it was to be placed in the walls. The government furnished goggles to protect workmen's eyes and work was started. Requiring the hardest steel for chisels, they found it in discarded automobile axles. To each building was assigned a forge and blacksmith. Sharpening chisels is a necessary phase of the work.[37]

Local architects were skillful in both styles: art deco and picturesque WPA rustic fieldstone. The careers and Depression era experiences of architects, landscape designers, and local builders help us appreciate the skill and care invested in these buildings by North Dakota architects like Gilbert Horton, Ritterbush Brothers, Edwin Molander, Ed Leonhard, Joseph Bell DeRemer and Samuel Teel DeRemer, William F. Kurke, Marius Houkom, and Theodore Wells. Academically trained landscape architects from outside the state like Ray F. Wyrick and Weldon Gratton brought a new disciplinary expertise to the design of local landscapes. Consider once more the emphasis that was given

---

[35] *Fargo Forum*, May 9, 1937.

[36] "The WPA in Minnesota," *Fargo Forum*, 1937.

[37] *Fargo Forum*, January 31, 1937.

on so many of these projects to innovative high-quality design. Oftentimes today, when we are faced with trying to accomplish building projects with insufficient resources, design is one of the first things to be jettisoned as an unnecessary frill or expendable extra. Well-designed Depression era buildings laid the groundwork for some impressive architectural careers that lasted several decades and produced hundreds of buildings. The projects also did a great deal to elevate the standard of public expectations for quality design on things like schools and hospitals and even civic or governmental office buildings.

Modeled after military efficiency, discipline, and physical effort for the common good, the Civilian Conservation Corps is the single most universally appreciated New Deal program.[38] Shortly after he took the oath of office as the 32nd president of the United States, FDR presented a message to Congress on the topic of unemployment relief. Mindful that the unemployed work force nationally had risen from 3 percent in 1929 to over 25 percent in 1933, Roosevelt suggested an immediate plan to enroll unemployed persons in public work.[39] Among the prioritized projects were conservation and development of natural resources, including control, utilization, and purification of water, prevention of erosion, development of water power, transmission of electrical energy, flood control, and improvements to drainage and rivers.

Roosevelt proposed to establish a program to "enlist young unemployed men in an army" to work on federal public lands doing forestry, preventing soil erosion, controlling both floods and drought, and similar resource conserving projects. In his message he stated:

> I have proposed to create a civilian conservation corps to be used in simple work, not interfering

[38]John A. Salmond, *The Civilian Conservation Corps 1933–1942: A New Deal Case Study* (Durham, NC: Duke University Press, 1967), 54, 218.
[39]John C. Paige, *The Civilian Conservation Corps and the National Park Service, 1933–1942* (Washington, DC: National Park Service and U.S. Government Printing Office, 1985), 3–5.

> with the normal employment, and confining itself to forestry, the prevention of soil erosion, flood control, and similar projects . . . The type of work is of definite, practical value, not only through the prevention of great financial loss, but also as a means of creating future national wealth . . . Control of such work can be carried on by executing machinery of the Departments of Labor, Agriculture, War and Interior. The enterprise will . . . conserve our precious natural resources and more important will be the moral and spiritual gains of such work.[40]

Rather than establish a new federal bureaucracy, responsibility for the CCC program was divided among four existing cabinet departments: Labor, War, Interior, and Agriculture. The Department of Labor initiated a nationwide recruiting program for screening and selecting enrollees. The Department of War was responsible for providing medical exams; organizing enrollees into companies; constructing the CCC camps; housing, feeding, clothing, training, and providing benefits to the enrollees. The Department of the Interior was in charge of directing work projects within the National Parks, as well as operations of the Office of Education, the Bureau of Indian Affairs, and the Bureau of Reclamation. The Park Service and Forest Service, known together as the "technical services," were responsible for the actual work projects, technical planning and execution, and supervision of the work force. The Department of Agriculture was responsible for projects associated with the US Forest Service and the Soil Conservation Service. The Forest Service coordinated projects on state and private lands as well as those in the national forests.[41]

Conservation projects focused on erosion control and water conservation. North Dakota was one of only a few states in which these conservation projects were a substantial part of WPA

---

[40]FDR "Message to Congress," March 1933.

[41]Perry H. Merrill, *Roosevelt's Forest Army: A History of the Civilian Conservation Corps, 1933–1942* (Montpelier, VT: Perry H. Merrill, 1981), 7–8.

Typical Depression era water impoundment constructed by CCC crews near Lankin, on the upper reaches of the Forest River.
Photograph provided courtesy of Keith Bylin.

accomplishments. In some instances, WPA continued work that had been initiated by CCC companies (since WPA was less restrictive in the employment of local labor) and continued the program of dam construction in drought areas of the state. Small dams (including farm livestock dams) were generally earthen and stone riprap construction, while more elaborate larger dams made extensive use of concrete and stonework. Erosion control also included terracing and construction of check dams and irrigation drainage channels. The North Dakota State Fish Hatchery at Valley City was substantially developed under WPA, and drainage improvements at numerous wildlife refuges were implemented.

In North Dakota, CCC enrollees were sent first to the statewide headquarters at Fort Abraham Lincoln in Bismarck (not to be confused with historic Fort Abraham Lincoln, south of Mandan). The initial enrollment of North Dakotans in the CCC consisted of

1,400 men in eight companies, who arrived at Fort Abraham Lincoln in August 1933. The first camps beyond the headquarters camp were established in June 1933 at Devils Lake, Minot, Williston, Bottineau, Dickinson, and Jamestown.[42] By 1937 there were 3,800 men employed in twenty North Dakota companies. The CCC Camps were assigned a designation by letters indicating, in a general way, their primary purpose or agency affiliation. Those most active in North Dakota dealt with soil conservation (including shelterbelts), water management, land reclamation, wildlife habitat, and erosion control, but also to some extent with improvement of state parks.

The CCC camps typically consisted of two hundred men, although there were occasionally a few smaller camps. An eventual total of fifty-six CCC camps (of varying sizes and duration) have been identified in North Dakota.[43] Originally, enrollees were housed in canvas tents, which were intended for all CCC camps. In most winters, the North Dakota companies received orders to relocate temporarily to wintering station camps in Minnesota, South Dakota, Arkansas, or California. Enrollees traveled by train to their new destinations and performed general camp work at those stations from October to April, at which time they returned by train to North Dakota. By 1934, twenty-four companies had been established in North Dakota.[44] It was reported in 1936 that fifty-one North Dakota CCC camp enrollees had met requirements for high school graduation through coursework completed in the camps. Forty-three other enrollees had satisfied eighth-grade graduation requirements. Many of the men were permitted to return to their hometowns on leave to graduate with their hometown graduating class.

---

[42]Consistent with the objective of relocating workers to the "healthful, rural countryside" (a debatable premise during the Dust Bowl), most camps were well outside major cities. When camps were later established near Fargo, Grand Forks, and Bismarck, they tended to utilize CCC-Veterans' companies.

[43]A map of North Dakota camp locations and company assignments is available at https://ccclegacy.org.

[44]North Dakota District CCC 7th Corps Area, "Official Annual, Civilian Conservation Corps, 1937," (Bismarck: 7th Corps Headquarters, 1937).

A CCC camp was situated near the southwest corner of Wishek where the "CC-boys" lived through "the worst dust storm in history" and accomplished local Soil Conservation Service work, including erosion control and shelterbelt planting. Working on behalf of the Soil Conservation Service, camps like SCS-1 near Wishek and SCS-2 near Mott mainly constructed small dams of rock and earth. Much of that work remains in place and functional in our present day. They also did important shelterbelt construction and tedious grasshopper extermination. The impact of the CCC on North Dakota was extraordinary, and benefits are still felt today. For nine years, the CCC program gave the state millions of man-days of critically necessary conservation labor, advancing the state's parks and soil conservation efforts. Critically-timed, professional studies of park design, wildlife resources, and management plans brought to bear a well-informed level of critical environmental judgment than would have been possible under any other circumstances.[45] Under the CCC, water-retention ponds and low-level dams improved water resource management, providing the basis for many successful agricultural irrigation practices through our present day. Because many of these so-called submarginal lands were so ill suited for agriculture or even for ranching, the CCC addressed the emergency problem of restoring idle lands for public recreation and resource conservation uses.

Work of the CCC camps implemented many of the first initiatives that addressed planned resettlement and environmentally sustainable landscape readjustment on the drought-prone Great Plains. Regionally, the goal of the shelterbelt program was to plant forty million trees in North Dakota, South Dakota, Nebraska, Kansas, Oklahoma, and Texas. For this purpose, a state nursery was established by the CCC, together with the US For-

[45]Kenneth E. Hendrickson, Jr., "Relief for Youth: The Civilian Conservation Corps and the National Youth Administration in North Dakota," *North Dakota History: Journal of the Northern Plains* 48, no. 4 (Fall 1981): 17–22.

est Service, in the Denbigh Dunes area of North Dakota.[46] This important work relief venture was a fundamental function of the Prairie States Forestry Project. The CCC "boys" built hundreds of modest but well-crafted buildings, erected 431,555 rods of fence, constructed 623,012 cubic yards of levees and water control features, 124 impoundment dams and 356 small reservoirs. Working in every part of the state they planted 1,773 acres of trees and shelterbelts and improved 8,625 acres of mature forest. Eventual control of soil erosion through installation of shelterbelts under the Conservation Service began with field labor initially undertaken by the CCC in most parts of the state. The CCC crews re-vegetated nearly seven thousand acres of range land and spent 2,762 man days fighting forest fires.

Overall, the effect of the CCC as a work relief agency was well received in North Dakota. The public was accepting of the CCC program because it treated minimal enrollee payment more as a stipend in exchange for regimented, supervised hard labor closely analogous to military service. Popularity was also helped by returning the majority of the worker's pay to benefit their families and home communities. Even the reaction of the press was generally favorable, as typified by a 1935 editorial in the *Grand Forks Herald*, acknowledging that Roosevelt's proposal to engage young men in productive labor, intelligently administered, could produce benefits of lasting value at a reasonable cost.[47] The CCC and WPA work relief wages yielded immediate benefit for families. Referred to as "dollar-a-day" men, the CCC workers earned thirty dollars a month (plus room and board) with the requirement that twenty-five of those dollars had to be sent home to families they were helping to support. Supervisors and "Local Experienced Men" were sometimes "36-ed," meaning that they earned an additional six dollars a month for leadership roles and re-

[46]Thomas J. Turck, "Denbigh Station and Experimental Forest National Historic District," National Register of Historic Places nomination, March 2010. The North Dakota State Review Board approved the nomination for submittal to the National Register.

[47]*Grand Forks Herald*, April 16, 1933, 5.

sponsibilities. Workers and families benefited similarly from WPA investment, earning $10.40 a week for up to one hundred hours per month.

It is not inconsequential that the experience gained by army officers in managing crews of enrollees at the CCC camps provided valuable training that was translated by the Department of War when the United States entered World War II. The context of work relief construction during the Great Depression demonstrates both the historical events and the unique circumstances of design and construction by the CCC companies. All these visionary social purposes were accomplished while providing educational benefits, skills training, and economic revitalizations to otherwise destitute men and their families. A large majority of all the features still in use today at North Dakota's state and national parks, state historic sites, national wildlife refuges, watersheds and riparian corridors resulted from the work relief enterprise of the CCC camps.[48]

With increasing awareness in the 1930s of erosion, drainage runoff, effects of drought, and degradation of habitat, a variety of conservation structures were built throughout North Dakota to manage grasslands, wildlife, and the state's water resources. The CCC initiated thirty major projects of this type and completed dozens of smaller dam features. Following up on those initiatives, the WPA alone was responsible for completing an additional ten conservation projects and involved destitute farmers as laborers to build several hundred smaller-scale dams for water impoundments in drought affected parts of the state. The dams were constructed using a variety of local earthen fill materials and rock when available.

The National Wildlife Refuges initially established in North Dakota in the 1930s have grown to be part of the largest and most extensive network of waterfowl habitat preserves in the world. The work was essentially undertaken to mitigate the ef-

[48]Neil M. Maher, *Nature's New Deal: The Civilian Conservation Corps and the Roots of the American Environmental Movement* (New York: Oxford University Press, 2008).

fects of drought, soil erosion, and degradation of wildlife habitat. The pivotal role of J. Clark Salyers II in establishing this system is recognized by the association of his name with a major wildlife refuge on the Upper Souris Waterfowl Refuge. At the Chase Lake National Wildlife Refuge, creeks were diverted to send their waters into the lake and an overflow channel was constructed on the southwest shore of the lake. Improvements and additions to state Fish Hatcheries at Valley City and Washburn were also sponsored by federal relief construction grants. Ponds were constructed and improved at both sites and new hatchery buildings were built. The original ponds and the resident headquarters building at Valley City National Fish Hatchery complex were constructed of local stone.

Conservation structures like these represent North Dakota's first large-scale, statewide effort to manage the state's natural resources. These efforts resulted in extensive improvement in the state's national grasslands, further development of state parks, the construction of numerous dams for the purposes of water conservation and recreation, the development of wildlife refuges and fish hatcheries, and the reduction of soil erosion through various conservation farming practices and planting of shelterbelts. Shelterbelt windbreaks were stands of trees strategically planted as part of the Prairie States Forestry Project to reduce wind erosion on farmland. Franklin D. Roosevelt was a strong advocate for the plan to mitigate wind erosion by planting a belt of trees some one-hundred-feet wide and extending from the Canadian provinces to Texas. The Prairie States Forestry Project was a regionally-planned land conservation strategy that took shape largely in the Dakotas, based on research initiated at the Denbigh Dunes State Experimental Forest near Towner by Dr. Joseph Stoeckeler. Much of the planting work for the shelterbelt component, still prominent on the landscape today, was accomplished utilizing CCC and WPA labor as well as work relief labor contributed by individual farmers.

Shelterbelts were planted on hundreds of farms and covered thousands of acres in the state. Because of the life expectancy of some of the species, it is understandable that examples of shelterbelts from this era still exist. Several particularly good, visible examples are located between Kindred and Enderlin along State Highway 46 along the boundary between Cass, Richland, and Ransom Counties. Many of the tree species have matured and are nearing the end of their viable lifespan after seventy years, thereby warranting the clearing of deadwood and replanting. North Dakota's shelterbelts are a remarkable feature of the rural landscape, and many are in serious need of renewal.

Other conservation efforts in North Dakota included projects aimed at managing wind and water erosion. Seventeen CCC com-

A typical North Dakota shelterbelt (windbreak) landscape near Enderlin, constructed by CCC crews under the auspices of the federal Prairie States Forestry Project.

panies, under the direction of the Soil Conservation Service, constructed drainage terraces, pasture furrows, irrigation ditches/ sod waterways, and contour lines for contour farming to reduce runoff. They also demonstrated strip cropping and rough tillage and planted several shelterbelts to reduce wind erosion. As past flood events in the Souris basin demonstrated, we are still living off much of the infrastructure from Depression era work relief construction projects.

The work relief programs invested in communities as a way of affirming their worth. Though perhaps not as glamorous as public buildings from an architecture historian's perspective, construction of modern public utilities was one of the most popular projects of the period. In fact, more than half of the projects funded by the Public Works Administration involved improvements in public utilities. These important projects have benefited North Dakota communities like Richardton, Steele, Killdeer and Watford City for several decades, and only now are some of them being replaced with more modern works of engineered functionality.

In communities and scattered rural settings where sewage treatment facilities were not feasible, federal relief programs (primarily the WPA) constructed sanitary privies to improve overall community sanitation and reduce the risk of various diseases. Privies were square or rectangular, depending on the number of seats, and usually had a shed or gable roof. The largest majority was wood frame, although concrete construction and modern sanitary materials were often used for floors and "pedestals." A small square window is a distinctive feature of WPA privies. More than 2.3 million sanitary privies were constructed nationwide, of which more than 32,000 were constructed in North Dakota. This significant public health achievement is documented in photos and design drawings among the promotional materials of the WPA. Though in most instances there is no longer pressing functional need for most outdoor privies, many of them continue to be maintained and preserved as a matter of local property owner interest.[49]

A remarkable body of Depression era architectural and landscape work are in evidence today in German-Russian Country. It is a compelling demonstration that CCC, WPA, and other work relief programs did a tremendous amount of social and environmental good. In our closeness to these communities, we continue to be impressed with how effectively these far-reaching programs changed the equation of social and economic depression and improved the nation's approach to scientifically managing policy for the environment, education, and civic infrastructure. Small-scale work relief projects did much good in rehabilitating neglected and abused environments: watersheds, public utilities, and wildlife habitats. The work relief programs were an expression of confidence in the belief that Americans could anticipate, plan, and moderate the effects of environment, economics, and human institutions. The building projects clearly raised the standard of public expectations for architectural design and for the quality of life people in small towns were entitled to expect. Work relief buildings and recreation amenities continue to enhance the quality of life and the spirit of cultural value in countless rural communities.

New Deal work relief programs established some of the first parameters for long-range land use planning and rural resettlement, as well as providing funding for the restoration of grasslands and wildlife refuges. Improved wildlife refuges have helped to mitigate the potential for environmental disaster on the arid, drought-prone northern plains. Programs like the CCC and National Youth Administration (NYA) afforded a kind of proving ground for subsequent recruitment, training, and enlistment of

---

[49]Privies have occasionally been recommended to the National Register as eligible properties, but to date none appears on the list of approved properties. The author has visited and photographed one well-maintained example of a WPA-approved modern privy on a farm outside the community of Great Bend in Richland County, but no documentary information is yet on the official public record.

young people in the military services. The ostensible purpose of the federal work relief construction projects was to provide economic opportunities for unemployed laborers. Statistical information substantiates the degree to which this objective was fulfilled. But the federal work relief programs implemented in North Dakota from 1931 to 1943 provided many other benefits as well. The investments made to create parks, playfields, and historic sites continue to benefit North Dakota citizens.

Many of the building projects were small, modest, incremental, and local, but through the quality of their architectural design and materials, historic buildings and landscapes in German-Russian Country suggest the cultural importance of work, self-reliance, and contribution of personal talents and labor. These enduring buildings—wonderful in their hand-crafted character and architectural sophistication—tempt us to value and appreciate the distinctive features of federal work relief construction statewide. Effectively, the federal work relief construction activities demonstrated modern scientific thinking as a strategy for renewing communities. Work relief projects established a reasonable expectation that life's hardships ought not be so severe if something modest could be done in the way of investment to improve local conditions.

In many dwindling North Dakota communities, the work relief construction projects were the last significant public investment in local infrastructure. Federal investment in small North Dakota communities in the 1930s affirmed that those places were meritorious enough to justify the basic amenities of civic life. The project "works" were important to spiritual renewal, but so was the work; the physical investment of effort and caring. People in truly dire need were treated with dignity. Communities were revived and renewed. A local sense of worth was restored and the social value of work was reaffirmed. In light of Harry Hopkins's proclamation that America is the richest country in the world, that we can afford to pay for anything we want, *and that we want a decent life for all the*

Interior detail of the powerful and architecturally ambitious laminated long span arches inside the Wishek Civic Auditorium. Designed by Gilbert R. Horton and constructed by local WPA workers.

Prairie Festival sessions are set to begin inside the Wishek Civic Auditorium. *Photo by Ken Schmierer.*

people in this country, surely this enduring body of architecture and design is worthy of our thoughtful attention and continued appreciation.

We understand best by taking time to appreciate with our own eyes and based on knowledge that local people have been willing to share about their communities. With passage of time, we are currently seeing some of the last opportunities to learn from firsthand personal experiences retold by unselfish, hardworking people who lived through these historical events. The work relief buildings in German-Russian Country are capable of speaking to us if we will give them a voice and allow those walls to talk. By examining buildings from a historical perspective, we can appreciate how much North Dakotans continue to care about their communities and architectural heritage, even beyond any tangible, useful value. North Dakotans continue believing the platitude from a WPA poster affirming "Work Builds Confidence." We know that human effort can make a positive difference in our quality of life. Good work is its own reward, and we are beneficiaries of a cultural heritage formed by people who truly understood the importance of productive work as one of the greatest spiritual virtues we are privileged to invest in future generations. North Dakota's work relief buildings tell a story about the importance of work in sustaining communities, affirming the social value of work to both the community and the worker. Work is life itself.

Refusing Nostalgia
Memory and Place in German-Russian Country

By Debra Marquart[1]

[1]Distinguished Professor of Liberal Arts and Sciences at Iowa State University, Debra Marquart teaches in ISU's MFA Program in Creative Writing and Environment. She was Poet Laureate of the State of Iowa from 2019 to 2024. Marquart hails from the town of Napoleon, deep in the heart of German-Russian Country. A form of this essay was first published in *The Night We Landed on the Moon: Essays Between Exile & Belonging* (NDSU Press, 2021).

The past is a foreign country: they do things differently there.

—L.P. Hartley

When I asked Grandma Geist about the village in South Russia where my grandfather had emigrated from (Grandpa was notoriously quiet so you had to direct all questions to Grandma Geist), she would say, "Oh, we all came from the same place." Hardly the stuff of legends.

I wanted the story of flight—the village he had left as a young boy under cover of darkness, the stale bread passed between many hands, the stony fields traversed in the middle of the night. I wanted the story of arrival—the storm-filled ocean passage, the train ride sluicing across the North American continent, the first sight of the muddy streets of Eureka, the early trading post town in the Dakota Territory where I knew through my research that our people had purchased carts and oxen to transport themselves to their remote land claims that lay yet farther north.

Instead, at gatherings where my grandparents would sit around and play cards with other couples they had known since youth, my grandmother might tell a joke in English and then turn to Grandpa and say the punch line to him, in German. All the old people would laugh and rock in their seats. When I protested—for I didn't know German, we were encouraged to learn only English—my grandmother would insist that it was only funny in German. "There's no way to say it, in English," she would explain.

Cultural amnesia—some small detour of meaning had occurred, something lost between the tongue and the brain. Even then, I felt myself cut loose on the ice floe of English. All the fun and forbidden stuff was happening in that other language that they spoke. But now that they are all long gone, I realize it was they who were drifting away on an ice floe of German. And I am left behind, a fully-vested American stranded without them on the mainland of English.

They had made homes for themselves, my earlier ancestors, in the new villages they created in South Russia in 1803, surviving the trauma of flight and exile from their own original homeland in Western Europe along the Rhine River. And they lived in those villages near the Black Sea as an ethnic minority for almost three generations. The promises they were given by the Czar—freedom from taxation, freedom from military service, the freedom to keep their own language, religions, and schools—held for about eighty years.

When some of those promises were withdrawn and young men from the villages were forcibly conscripted into the Russian military, waves of families began to flee Russia and immigrate to America. All of my German-Russian great-grandparents and their young children—my grandfathers among them—arrived in the US between the years of 1886 and 1911. Answering the invitation for free land through the Homestead Act, they repeated the pattern of flight, exile, and resettlement in the Dakota Territory. This ethnic group, now sprinkled throughout much of the central United States is called the German-Russians, a name that's fuzzy in its definitions and forever shaped by flux. While the migrations that mark my ethnic group are preserved in their hyphenations, the fact of their arrival in America was never codified into language—we never became the "German-from-Russia Americans," for example. Some stories are too complicated to tell.

As a young girl, growing up in the 1950s and '60s in North Dakota, I was only vaguely aware of this ethnic history, but even the whiff of trauma and uprootedness was glamorous, especially against the everyday sameness of our hemmed-in farming enclave. Although the place where I grew up, Napoleon, was a small midwestern town in America, it often felt eerily like an eighteenth-century European village that just happened to have televisions and automobiles. My grandfather made sausage and rhubarb wine in the basement. In the root cellar were rows of gleaming jars full of pickles and beets. Chores had to be done, and animals needed tending. My father's idea of a family outing was to pile us all into the car on Sunday evenings and drive us around to look at the crops.

In this village of my hometown, rotund old men sat around on park benches gossiping with each other in German, and whiskery grandmothers endlessly baked and canned and sewed and gardened. There was a lot of church-going and polka-dancing. The older people spoke an archaic dialect of German, mixed with a broken English. In the local cafes, along with American foods like roast beef or hamburgers and French fries on the menus were choices like knoephla soup, sauerkraut, and fleischkuekle.

They had little of the backward glance in them, my maternal grandparents. I would go so far as to say they refused nostalgia. The word "nostalgia" has its origins in Greek words, but not in Greek culture. Cobbled together from two Greek roots—nostos (meaning "return" or sometimes "journey") and algeo (meaning "pain," "sickness," or "sorrowful"), the term "nostalgia," was coined in 1688 by the Swiss Doctor, Johannes Hofer, to describe the "sad mood originating from the desire to return to native land." In *The Future of Nostalgia*, Svetlana Boym reports that Hofer first documented this phenomenon in various people displaced in the seventeenth century—"freedom loving students from the Republic of Berne studying in Basel, domestic help and servants working in France and Germany, and Swiss soldiers fighting abroad."

Dr. Hofer had observed that this new illness caused the afflicted to lose touch with the present resulting in their "longing for the native land to become their single-minded obsession." The patients' symptoms included a "lifeless and haggard countenance," an "indifference toward everything," and "a confusion between past and present, real and imaginary events."[2]

[2]Svetlana Boym, *The Future of Nostalgia* (Basic Books, 2001), 3.

According to Boym, Swiss scientists found that the simplest sensual cues of home, such as the tune of folk melodies of Alpine valleys were likely to trigger a "debilitating nostalgic reaction in Swiss soldiers." Military superiors were forced to prohibit the soldiers from playing, singing, or even whistling native tunes. Later cures for bouts of nostalgia were more severe. Boym reports that in 1733 when the Russian army was stricken with nostalgia just as it ventured into Germany, the commanding officers announced that the "first to fall sick [with nostalgia] would be buried alive," a practice which seemed to work as an immediate curative on the sufferer.[3]

In the case of all my great-grandparents and my two grandfathers, both of whom immigrated to the United States as young boys, I could theorize that the hardship of emigration and the privation they experienced after arrival was enough to shake the nostalgic impulse right out of them. But that remains a theory, because I have no records about the quality of their everyday lives—no letter collections, no journals, no family stories. In the absence of information and into that negative space, it's difficult to formulate a theory. Perhaps the silence speaks for itself.

When I go to the state archives for historical information about the early days of European settlement in Dakota Territory, I find that archival records do exist. Primary among them are the 1930s Works Progress Administration (WPA) records that employed writers to travel around counties in North Dakota and interview the remaining immigrant generation. A WPA interview form was utilized that asked general questions about family data (names/birthdates), along with details on date and year of passage, name of ship, cost of ticket, etc. A general prompt at the end of the interview form invited the interviewee to provide supplemental information in various categories such as "political events" (county seat fights, party caucuses, vigilantes), "social events" (weddings, dances, games), "industries" (trapping, soap

[3]Svetlana Boym, *The Future of Nostalgia* (Basic Books, 2001), 5.

making, picking buffalo bones), as well as a "miscellaneous" category that included "frost, hail, drought, cyclones, hoppers, blizzards, prairie fires, epidemics, Indian scares, claim jumpers, and etc."

The extensiveness and specificity of this final category leads one to assume there was a great deal of miscellaneous trouble to be found in the early days of the region. But what's even more striking about the WPA interview documents is the fact that while the interviews with Irish, English, German, Norwegian, and Swedish immigrants are often full of lively detail, the interviews with the German-Russian immigrants tend to be shorter and filled with cursory details. One WPA worker jots a field observation at the end of a report: "I can get very little information from this couple. When I ask them what they do in their leisure time, they reply they have no leisure time . . . I can only assume they believe me to be an insurance salesman."[4]

All the WPA interviewees were invited to include a supplemental narrative relaying additional anecdotes about early pioneer life. These were appended to the back of the formal WPA interview report. Perhaps it goes without saying that most of the German-Russian interviews do not include additional material. By contrast, one loquacious interviewee, Peter Borr, who lists Michigan, Holland, and The Netherlands as the origin points of his family's multiple migrations, takes the opportunity to include a forty-eight page "Pioneer History," with subject headings as various as the "History of the Van Raalte Reformed Church," "Our Married Life," "Our Post Immigration Condition," "Home Construction in the Early Days," "Our Financial Experiences: The Ups and Downs," a "Political Horoscope from 1876," and a poem authored by Mr. Borr himself.

The most stunning section of this WPA interview document, however, features an eight-page report titled, "North Dakota Sudden Deaths," in which Mr. Borr has taken it upon himself to note

[4]WPA Interview Archives, 1939.

the details of 207 sudden or unusual deaths, such as the following, all of which occurred in the region between the years of 1886 and 1936.

> 1886: John Robinson shot by Carlson near Apple Creek.
>
> 1888: Bollinger kills self out of fear of arrest for not paying debts.
>
> 1891: James Findley shoots wife, then self to death near Winchester.
>
> 1888: Grens frozen to death east of Mound City.
>
> 1896: Young man killed by lightning while cultivating corn near Gackle.
>
> 1889: C. Hanson shoots his head off near Hull.
>
> 1898: Mrs. Reynolds found dead in shallow pond, shortly after Mr. Reynolds was found shot through the heart, lying on a log at Omio.
>
> 1913: L. Tinholt mysteriously disappears at his opera house, while it burns.
>
> 1927: Son of Mitchell dragged to death by pony nine miles north of Herried.
>
> 1929: J.J. Fenelon shoots self at Pollock.
>
> 1929: Becthold shot dead at Mobridge.
>
> 1923: Three children freeze to death under sleigh as they returned from school in storm.
>
> 1918: Jack Bickle dies from Dr. Till's treatments.
>
> 1924: M. Bickle crushed under wagon at Artas.
>
> 1920: C. Vorlander shoots self on daughter's grave at Eureka.[5]

Just this sampling of the death entries, simply stated in one-line summaries, reveals the violence, hardship, and trauma of the early days. Although my great-grandparents were immigrants and my grandparents were children and young adults during these years, none of these stories were told or referenced as vague memories by the time I was growing up near or around

[5]Peter Borr, "Accidental and Sudden Deaths," Supplemental Report, Emmons County WPA Interview Archives, 6 November 1939.

the very places where these tragedies occurred. In fact, you wouldn't have had a clue (as I did not) that the older people of these towns had known and lived through harsh times. As I read these reports, I can only conclude that they were engaged in a profound and willful act of repression and silencing, an immaculate execution of cultural amnesia.

Instead of dwelling on the dead and the past, it seems they turned their attentions forward to us, their grandchildren, and outward, to the land itself. "Never let the land go out of the family." This is a caution I heard often and always growing up. As the owners of the center farm, the original homestead, my family has become the caretaker of a legacy that's important, if only conceptually, to cousins and uncles and aunts who live in places far and wide.

But what makes a piece of land go solid under your feet, especially to people with a multi-generational pattern of uprooting and migrating? How to explain this attachment to land that overtakes otherwise pragmatic people? "Archaic man saw settled land as sacred and the wilderness as profane," Mircea Eliade observed in *The Myth of the Eternal Return.*[6] Wilderness or uncultivated regions, to the mind of immigrants, were part of the undifferentiated void, something that called out to be shaped and molded to their needs.

Eliade theorizes that when our ancestors performed rites of cultivation such as plowing, seeding, and finally inhabiting a piece of land, they saw themselves as "cosmicizing" it and making it sacred by matching its physical shape to the cosmic model or ideal that existed if only in their imaginations. According to Eliade, people who settled unbroken land for cultivation believed themselves to be performing something akin to an act of creation. Like God, they were doing elemental things—separating the light from the dark, the earth from the sky, the land from the ocean. They were making order from chaos.

---

[6]Mircea Eliade, *The Myth of the Eternal Return* (Princeton University Press, 1954), 10.

At that moment, according to Eliade, no matter how difficult the work they felt their lives take on a greater resonance. Their actions connected them to ancient, ongoing patterns—what Eliade described as a "ceaseless repetition of gestures"—and through these gestures they felt their connection to a chain of being that stretched far back in time beyond themselves to known and unknown ancestors.[7]

Family land, by association, then becomes the locus, the site that records the sacrifices and successes of our ancestors. All the details of the people and the hardships become conflated across centuries, folded in, tucked away, and eventually forgotten by succeeding generations. After that general forgetting is complete, only the *fact* of the land remains, a geographical reminder connecting us to all those who came before.

This fusion of home and land in the minds of those who remain is often expressed in Willa Cather's *O Pioneers!* People are fleeting and ephemeral, she observes, but the land holds the future. "How many of the names on the county clerk's plat will be there in fifty years?" Cather writes. "We come and go, but the land is always here. And the people who love it and understand it, are the people who own it—for a little while."[8]

Whatever sentimentality I may have observed in my grandparents about land or people, may be more accurately defined as Heimat, a German concept that's equally as complex as nostalgia, but even more problematic. Heimat can mean an attachment to homeland, abode, landscape, or habitat. But its meaning is also elusive and has been reinterpreted for political ends, especially to justify excluding populations deemed by the majority not to "belong" to a particular landscape.

At its core, Helen Thomas explains in her article, "Colonizing the Land," the concept of Heimat, describes a sense of integrity or wholeness in a place, "a feeling of belonging together in one place, a feeling of being at home." But it's also an illusion. "Hei-

[7]Mircea Eliade, *The Myth of the Eternal Return* (Princeton University Press, 1954), 5.
[8]Willa Cather, *O Pioneers!* (Book of the Month Club, 1996), 308.

A homecoming: Logan County author Debra Marquart details the joys and longings of a native daughter of German-Russian Country—addressing the Prairie Places Festival from the show ring of the Napoleon Livestock arena. *Photo by Ken Schmierer.*

Debra Marquart speaks to a full house in the Napoleon Livestock auction arena, a symbol of thriving livestock husbandry in German-Russian Country. *Photo by Suzzanne Kelley.*

mat is such that if one would go closer and closer to it, one would discover that at the moment of arrival it is gone. It has dissolved into nothingness."[9]

And so as I try to approach describing it, the ache for that place I was born to and these people I was bound to—whole generational waves of family members who have disappeared from my view—the ache only increases even as the image fades. And finally I realize that I am the one who suffers most acutely from nostalgia, not only from the loss of that feeling of belonging or Heimat that they created for me as a child, but also from regret that the illusion of home they presented felt so solid and claustrophobic to me as a child that all I could do was bristle against it, then engineer my escape, sealing my separation from the people and place that now as an adult I am compelled to haunt in my imagination, returning again and again.

Perhaps this is just the natural condition of aging and loss. My grandparents had the doubly complex dilemma of having a past that was not only figuratively a foreign country—the natural foreign country that all childhoods are when we glance back at them from the far distance of our later years—but also a past that was literally a foreign country, one about which they did not seem to have memory or language to share with us. And so I experience nostalgia for them in multiple layers—ache for my own foreign country of childhood and ache for all the foreign countries of their unique history that disappeared unarticulated and unrecorded in my grandparents' foreign tongues.

Now I spend my time searching through old newspapers, written in languages I do not know, through letter collections and archives in quiet library aisles. I visit graveyards, nursing homes. I smile at old people I see in the street, hoping they will tell me something about the old days. I have an obsessive habit of scanning the faces of modern-day refugees I see in news

---

[9]Helen Thomas, "Colonizing the Land: Heimat and the Constructed Landscapes of Mexico's Ciudad Universitaria," Felipe Hernandez, editor, *Transculturation* (Leiden, Netherlands: Brill, 2008), 110.

reports on CNN, hoping to get a glimpse of the familiar, a long-lost grandparent.

Most of the time it's sad and lonely work, this reclamation of the past, and then sometimes you get lucky. A few years ago, when I was doing research for *The Horizontal World: Growing Up Wild in the Middle of Nowhere,* my memoir about growing up a rebellious farmer's daughter on a North Dakota wheat farm, I visited older relatives and asked them questions about the old days. Usually, my questions were met with the same silences and suspicions as the WPA workers likely faced when they traveled around for the interview project in the 1930s.

Then one day, during a very ordinary conversation at my older cousin, Tony's, kitchen table, he began to tell me about the milk letters he remembered that had come for my great-grandfather from the brothers and sisters he had left behind in the Black Sea villages when they fled.

Tony was only a boy at the time, but he remembered that the letters from Russia were written in two layers, the first of which was visible to the eye, penned in ink or pencil, reporting mundane news from the village (births, natural deaths, weddings). Well into the 1920s, my great-grandfather received these letters from those he had left behind in Russia. By then, he was a prosperous North Dakota landowner, but the news from Russia only grew more troubling.

The second layer of the letter, Tony said, was invisible and written in milk between the ink lines. Blown dry on the breath of the worried author as if to make it undetectable to the eyes of the government censors, this second layer, the milk letter, recounted the horrors of life under Communism. It begged for money and detailed reports of mass starvation and farm collectivization in the region of my great-grandfather's home village.

The milk letter told of peasant uprisings, grave robbing, church stripping, and of sons and fathers herded up and taken either to servitude in the Russian military or to forced labor camps in Siberia. These are all events now documented in more

Generational conversation: Gladys Marquart and her literary daughter, Debra, at Napoleon Livestock. *Photo by Ken Schmierer.*

formal histories that we know befell those from our ethnic group who stayed behind in the villages in Russia.

Tony remembers my great-grandfather sitting on a stool in front of the north window of our farmhouse, a stream of tears flowing down his otherwise stoic face, as he held the shaking letter up to the sunlight to illuminate the lines written in milk. A few years later, Tony recalls, in the early 1930s, the letters stopped coming and all talk of Russia ceased.

I grew up in that farmhouse in the 1960s. I sat at that north window, most often scanning the highway for the bus or for the carload of friends that was coming to take me for some adventure in town. As I grew up, one road led to another, all of them away and into the future. But I'm ready now to take up my spot at that window, to hold everything up to the fiercest light, to report the invisible layers of stories I find hidden there.

Dinosaurs on the Prairie (a trail of threshing machines) is one of the sites to be seen near Marquart's hometown of Napoleon.
Photo by Suzzanne Kelley with permission of Reagan Ann Caraway.

The German-Russian Voice

By Carol Just[1]

[1]Carol Just is a memory keeper, historian, and preservationist, and the mover and shaker behind the publication of *Watermelons and Thistles: Growing Up German from Russia in America* (Amber Skye Publishing, 2018). Here, she responds to the preceding chapters of *History & Memory in German-Russian Country* and considers the emergence of a German-Russian identity and voice and its grounding in landscape and space.

Funny how identity and voice, landscape and place follow a person on their life journey. I might not have known my heritage was unique if my parents, uncles, and aunts hadn't left McIntosh County in southcentral North Dakota in the 1930s and early 1940s to farm a couple of counties to the east—taking them out of the German-Russian Country—Sauerkraut Triangle. The three families farmed near one another in LaMoure County and over time became immersed in community and church. In conversation with one another they maintained their German language, and my mother and aunts maintained the delicious foodways of our culture. Beyond that, we were immersed in the melting pot of cultures. Our parents seemed to like it that way. They encountered some stinging prejudice in their first years in LaMoure County and didn't want their children to experience the same.

Our LaMoure County neighbors were a grand mix of old-stock Americans, second and third generation northern European descendants and a myriad of religions. They were all good folks embracing Judeo-Christian values. It was a good life. Our families were well respected as farmers and were engaged in civic as well as religious activities. We children thrived, received a good education and fine leadership opportunities. We will always consider our Just Farm and Berlin, North Dakota, our first home.

As the youngest of the LaMoure County cousins, I usually accompanied my parents when they went back to McIntosh County to visit their huge extended family. Over time I began to notice a pattern. While my parents left their first geography, Frieda and Strasburg Townships in McIntosh County for economic reasons—no land available for purchase and they didn't want to rent land for the rest of their lives—their return visits almost always brought out a happiness and joy that I didn't see mirrored in our home community life. They chattered away in their dialect, worshipped in the German language at their old rural church on the prairie, picnicked with old friends and relatives along Beaver Creek, and seemed so relaxed and comfortable. They were clearly immersed in their identity and voice and grounded in landscape and place.

Over time I learned that language wasn't the only difference from my community in LaMoure County. There were also cultural and social differences in humor, jokes just sounded funnier in the German language; in song, theirs was a culture of singing at home, in church, and at picnics, and accordion music seemed to be everywhere; in dancing, they could work hard in the fields all day, do barn chores, eat, clean up and head to the nearest dance hall, dance until midnight or later and be up early the next morning to start all over again.

As a teen I spent a summer or two in McIntosh County helping an aunt and uncle as a "summer girl," caring for the younger children so my aunt could help in the fields. That time cemented my love of the German-Russian culture. While I never really grasped the nuance of the language and rarely translated quickly enough to catch on when an uncle might be teasing me in German, I fell in love with the community, making it my second home.

My first real "ah ha" moment came in the early 1970s when my maternal grandfather shared his photograph collection with me and began to explain the family migration. I remember being stunned by the story of his ancestors' cross-continental movement from Alsace in Middle Europe to South Russia on the Black Sea and less than one hundred years later, a journey back across Europe to embark on an ocean voyage to the Port of New York before putting down roots in Dakota Territory.

Things began to make sense. I always wondered why our foodways more closely resembled Jewish or Ukrainian delicatessen food. Halupsi and borscht are not foods one associates with typical German cuisine. Words like *bashtan* or *halvah* are definitely not part of the standard German lexicon.

Grandpa knew what he was doing. He died shortly after his gift of photographs and memories, but he knew that if he gave me a taste of our history I would need to know more. I began reading anything and everything about the Germans from Russia. The writings of Adolph Schock, Joseph Height, Richard Sallet, Monsignor Aberle, Nina Farley Wishek, Adam Geisinger, and Karl Stumpp gave me a framework. I joined international organizations of Germans from Russia and attended annual conferences where I developed friendships with fellow researchers and attended classes and workshops.

Over the years, interest in my pioneer German-Russian heritage often took me to the rural North Dakota churches and cemeteries of my pioneer ancestors, usually with my mother and father, an aunt or uncle in tow. My companions supplied the detail that only family lore can provide. As Jessica Clark's research demonstrates earlier in this book, cemetery walks are especially useful in triggering memories of family relationships, religious devotion, funerals, and healthcare.

I became a fixture in county courthouses as I pored over dusty Clerk of Court and Register of Deed documents. My research began long before the advent of the internet so I had the delicious, sensory experience of touching the documents signed by my brave, amazing pioneering ancestors, making them real to me, not just data on a genealogy chart or an image in a photograph.

Going through birth and death records was equally sobering when I read the country doctor's assessment of the cause of death or realized that the report of death was often recorded months after the event by a relative who made a rare visit to the county seat. That explained why county records were often at odds with church records or even family Bible records.

I relied on oral interviews with great-aunts and great-uncles (the children of my emigrant ancestors) to help connect the dots.

My Germans-Russian relatives are a modest lot and my interviewees usually began with this disclaimer, "I really don't think I know much." What I learned is that many were simply waiting to be asked. Those interviews were the cornerstone of my research. Most of my interviewees kindly let me page through their family photo albums and Bibles, allowing me full access and permission to copy anything I wanted.

As Clark points out in her essay, "the new German-Russian story—is a story of hardships, as well as happiness." I learned that photographs were great memory triggers for my interviewees, bringing to the surface memories of past events that they hadn't thought about in years; memories that may have been buried with them had I not been in the right place at the right time. Those interviews blew life into my family history as I matched the

Carol Just, on site at the St. Andrew's Church, planning and working on the preservation projects of the buildings and the upkeep of the cemetery. *Photo by Suzzanne Kelley.*

names on the tombstones to the stories and photographs that were shared with me and the official documents I found in the county courthouses. The US Bureau of Land Management supplied copies of homestead documents, proving that, even then, there was plenty of paperwork involved.

I'm often asked to give presentations about our German-Russian history and culture. I relish those opportunities to revisit the research I started all those years ago. Much of the research is anchored in my ancestral churches and the cemeteries in rural McIntosh County: Andreas Gemeinde, organized in 1893 by fifteen families who emigrated from the Glückstal Colonies in South Russia, now known as St. Andrew's Lutheran, and Friedens Gemeinde, which later became known as Peace Lutheran.

Church records show that after several years of worshipping in one another's homes, on October 18, 1892, it was decided to build a church home on Section 1, Township 130, Range 73 in McIntosh County. Land was donated by one of the original fifteen families. Sandstone was quarried from a bluff about twelve miles northwest of the building site and transported by horses pulling stone boats. The structure is rectangular, twenty-nine feet by twenty-two feet. The walls are approximately twenty-four inches thick, constructed of sandstone slices held together by a mortar of clay, straw, and water. Interior and exterior walls were originally finished with a render composed of the same mortar mixture used to bond the stone. Years later, commercial cement was overlain and whitewashed. Each charter member agreed to contribute fifteen days of labor, plus horses and wagons as required to carry the stone to the building site. Lumber for the roof, floor, and windows was purchased; the cost of the building totaled $385. The building was dedicated on March 21, 1883. By 1895, the congregants were able to retain a permanent pastor at an annual salary of $250. These young pioneers longed for their homes in South Russia and wished they could recreate the beautiful cathedral-like churches they remembered from their life on the steppe. The best they could do on the prairie was to build, with care and devotion, a larger version of a typical house in their home village—a stone house of worship.

For decades, Andreas Gemeinde was known as the "mother church" of a five-point parish that included Friedens, St. James, St. John, and St. Paul, all country churches located within a few miles of one another. Of the five churches, only Andreas Gemeinde, the original stone church built in 1893, standing next to the tall, wooden church, named St. Andrew's Lutheran, built in 1906, stand today. As Steve Martens writes in his chapter, "Great Depression Buildings and the Social Value of Work,"

> One of the important, durable values we can associate with the heritage of German-Russians is that when they build or improve something, they intend to make it last, which includes an unending responsibility to care for the upkeep and maintenance.

Both the 1893 stone church and the 1906 tall white, Carpenter Gothic style church are listed on the National Register of Historic Places. The 1906 structure was a recipient of a Preservation North Dakota grant in 2011, to help replace a leaky roof.

When I stroll through and do a cemetery count, I come up with more than fifty relatives buried in the St. Andrew's and Friedens cemeteries. Sixteen are great-great- grandparents, great-grandparents, and grandparents. Twenty-one more are great-uncles, great-aunts, aunts, and uncles. At least ten members of my family are buried in the children's sections. It makes sense to me that the voices in my head are especially loud when I'm there or in the old sanctuaries where my ancestors were baptized, confirmed, married, and buried.

While some people in the cemeteries lived to a ripe old age, others died young from common realities of pioneer life: epidemics, farm accidents, or childbirth. In Friedens cemetery alone, there are twenty-two children under the age of one year buried there. My uncle Otto Dockter, born and raised in McIn-

Plastered interior of the rock-and-gumbo old St. Andrew's Church, with window wells revealing the thickness of the old stone walls. *Photo by Ken Schmierer.*

A display cut-out in the St. Andrew's Church wall reveals how sandstone slices were held together with a mortar of clay, straw, and water in 1893. *Photo by Carol Just.*

tosh County, North Dakota, lost his life in Europe in the final months of WWII, less than a day's drive from the Alsace village his great-grandparents left in 1816 when they migrated to Neudorf in South Russia. His remains are buried in the American Cemetery in Luxembourg, but his family placed a marker in St. Andrew's cemetery to keep his memory close.

The names on the cemetery markers read like the roster of the founding members of the Glückstal Colonies (Glückstal, Neudorf, Bergdorf, and Kassel) in South Russia, who began settlement there in 1804.

McIntosh County in Dakota Territory opened for homestead in 1884 and was settled mostly by descendants of the Glückstal Colonies in South Russia. On the far western edge of the county, spilling into Emmons County, emigrants from the Kutschurgan Colonies of Baden, Kandel, Elsass, Strassburg, Selz, and Mannheim, as well as some colonies in Bessarabia, made their homes. All had been located within one hundred or so miles from Odessa on the Black Sea.

The earliest markers in St. Andrew's cemetery date back to 1894 and belong to a forty-nine-year-old mother and to three small children from three different families. They were casualties of the raw, unrelenting prairie life with its extreme heat and cold, isolation and illnesses that even the respected Brauchere, gifted healers trained in South Russia, found beyond the realm of their healing ability. A smallpox epidemic in the winter of 1898–99 claimed many on the prairie including three children of my great-grandparents, Adam and Magdalena Grusie Meidinger. The children died within three short weeks. Suddenly, their family was cut in half. The Spanish influenza epidemic of 1918–19 brought many more new graves to these rural cemeteries, and the diphtheria epidemic of 1923 cut to the core, claiming my grandfather, Karl Just, and three of his daughters, as well as his sister, Christina Just Thurn, and her three sons.

Iron crosses are a distinct cultural art form of the Germans from Russia. Most examples appear in cemeteries affiliated with the Catholic Church. However, the oldest marker in Friedens Cemetery is a large, ornate, hand-forged iron cross labeled Gottlieb Dockter. An emigrant from Neudorf, South Russia, Dockter spoke several languages and served as the Clerk of Court (*Schreiber*) for his village until he came to the United States with his family in 1889. With many sons to do the farm work, Dockter often roamed the prairie for days on horseback, always delighted when he connected with others from the colonies in South Russia. One day he stopped at a sod house near Beaver Creek and encountered a childhood friend, Johann Heine. As a young man, Heine migrated south of Neudorf to Klöstitz, in Bessarabia. Their reunion in McIntosh County, Dakota Territory, resulted in the marriage of Heine's daughter, Katharina, and Dockter's son, Jacob. Mergers of that kind were common in the early years on the prairie. As for the iron cross, the artist left no identification, but the fact that Dockter's son George was a well-known area blacksmith makes the case for a son creating a tribute to his father.

In the middle of all those cemetery markers with German surnames is a marker for a lone Norwegian emigrant by the name of Frank B. Olson. His homestead along Beaver Creek was surrounded by German-Russians. Olson married Carolina Heine, but left her a widow shortly after the marriage. He was buried on the homestead next to his father-in-law, Johann Heine. In 1910, both graves were exhumed, and the remains were moved to nearby St. Andrew's cemetery when a county road was platted in the path of their resting place.

In German-Russia culture, the cemetery (*Friedhof*) is a place of peace and dignity, meticulously cared for and located near the church building. As a migrating people, death was a reality of life. Assured of a life hereafter, German-Russians grieved the loss but placed their hope on the promise that they would meet again in heaven. For most emigrant families, a visit to the Friedhof in their native village in South Russia was the last stop for prayers

Sample of a hand-forged iron cross, marking the grave of Gottlieb Dockter. Located in Friedens Cemetery. *Photo by Carol Just.*

Close-up of the intricate detail on the Gottlieb Dockter iron cross. *Photo by Carol Just.*

and a mournful farewell before they embarked on their journey to America.

St. Andrew's, the tall white church, became known as a Beacon on the Prairie. When a church member died, the pastor or an elder of the congregation climbed the narrow steps to the bell tower and tolled the church bell the number of years the deceased lived on earth, honoring the life of the congregant and as a vehicle to notify the community, a practice that came with the emigrants from South Russia and continues with many congregations today.

In the early years before funeral homes were established, the deceased was laid out in the family parlor, usually in a hand-crafted wooden casket. Relatives and friends kept vigil by the casket until the funeral service. Funerals were a serious matter and attended by all in the community. Children were not sheltered from the grim reality of death. The procession from the sanctuary to the cemetery was a solemn one, sometimes with flower girls leading the pallbearers to the grave site. A lone voice began a graveside song, joined by all in attendance. "Wo Findet die Seele die Heimat, die Ruh" (Where does the soul find its home, its rest?) or "So Nimm Den Meine Hande" (Lord, take my hand and lead me) were common choices for adults; "Müde bin ich, geh zu Ruh" (Weary am I, to rest I go) was a lullaby often sung at the grave of a child. Many of these graveside traditions continue in McIntosh County today.

Ship records and homestead records show that the Germans from Russia, especially in the last two decades of the nineteenth century, came to America and homesteaded in large groups, allowing them to recreate the life they knew in South Russia on the North and South Dakota plains and Canadian prairies. As retired North Dakota State University Professor and noted Germans from Russia historian, Dr. Tim Kloberdanz, states, "The Germans from Russia were able to think globally and act locally." Meaning they could emigrate en mass to another part of the world and retain their community life in the new geography. There was, however, one very large difference.

The Homestead Act, signed by President Lincoln in 1862, mandated that homesteaders live on their acreage. No longer would the Germans from Russia enjoy the rhythm of village life. That mandate was hardest on the pioneer women who were accustomed to the mentorship and support of their mothers and grandmothers within the framework of village life. In South Russia, fields and pastures fanned out from the villages. In the planting, haying, or harvest seasons the farmers often made camp at the various fields, but most of the year came back into the villages at night. Village life was central to their existence. The orderly German villages in Russia were laid out in such a fashion that the marketplace in the center of the village was the hub of life. Homes had courtyards and walled fences with benches in front on a sidewalk lined with trees. Everyone could walk to the marketplace or the church located in the center of the village. Schools were usually located near the church and education was mandated and taught in the German language until Czar Alexander II eliminated their colonial status and deemed his German subjects become "Russified." It was that action by Czar Alexander II that prompted the exodus of the German-Russians to America and Canada.

North American ports in Nova Scotia, Maryland, and Texas were popular ports of entry. The busiest was Castle Garden in the Port of New York, located in Battery Park at the southern tip of Manhattan Island. Ellis Island, located off shore, opened in 1893 requiring ships to stop there so the new immigrants could be subject to a thorough examination before boarding a train taking them west. Most knew only a few English words, Dakota, potato, ticket, yes and no. In the case of my ancestors, three sets of my great grandparents traveled together from their village of Kassel to Dakota Territory in October 1884. Of the party of three families and two single men, the oldest was just thirty-years-old, and most had never traveled more than a few miles from their small village in South Russia.

The sea voyage was trying. They traveled in steerage, in the bowel of the ship, because it was the cheapest fare. My paternal great-grandparents, Christof and Elizabeth (Wanner) Just lost their infant son, Karl, to illness on the journey. He was buried at sea. These young adventurers spent that winter in a settlement called Tripp, near the territorial capital of Yankton, where a sister of one of the travelers had settled in an earlier migration in 1873.

By the spring of 1885, my great-grandparents were eager to dig their own roots in this new country. Land became available in McIntosh County, Dakota Territory, just north of what is now South Dakota. After purchasing their teams of oxen, wagons, and livestock, they loaded everything onto box cars and headed for the end of the line at Ipswich, near present day Aberdeen, South Dakota. Wives and children stayed with German-Russians already settled in the area while husbands made their way to the land office in Hoskins, near present-day Ashley. On May 21, 1885, the first of the Beaver Creek residents filed their Declaration of Intention papers to become US citizens, which allowed them to immediately file their homestead claims. Joyously the men returned to Ipswich to gather their families and possessions and begin a new life.

The first priority was to erect a shelter for the families. A makeshift hut was assembled from boards they purchased in Ipswich. They needed that hut, for the first month on the Dakota prairie they experienced a surprise May blizzard. Using oxen, the sod was broken and blocks were stacked on top of one another, just as a stone mason would build a brick house. Mud kept the blocks together and filled the cracks. For heating, they built stoves out of clay and stone, just as they used in South Russia. Life was hard. Everyone toiled. There was the never-ending task of clearing the land, gathering fuel at the creek bank, cutting hay for the livestock, and breaking the virgin sod. Sometimes the prairie grass could have roots ten to twenty feet deep. It was the German-Russians who perfected the breaking plow that cleared much of America's prairie. Children were dispatched to clear the land of rocks and pick up the millions of buffalo bones scattered across the prairie. The bones were hauled to the nearest railway station and sold for seven dollars a ton. They were quite literally the settlers' first crop.

Loneliness and isolation are common themes in my oral history research. The mandate that homesteaders live on their acreage made life much harder. They took strength from the fact that only a few generations before them, their ancestors had taken a similar leap of faith to settle the virgin steppe of South Russia at the invitation of Czar Alexander I. The promise of colonial status, meaning they could be self governing and keep their language and religion, was a major draw, as was the promise of freedom from conscription, meaning their sons would be exempt from the draft. The emigrants to America knew it could be done. Not without hardship, but that hadn't stopped their forebearers, and it didn't stop them.

For many years, acting locally worked for my pioneer ancestors. They were a kind of incubator of language and culture. Linguists today delight in the discovery of their language intact since the eighteenth century. While language evolved in Germany, especially after unification, the German language speakers who left Alsace, Rhineland Pfalz, Baden-Württemberg, and Prussia carried their dialects to Russia and later to North America mostly untouched except for the words they adopted in Russia.

German-Russians in Canada, North and South Dakota, especially, were able to maintain their ethnic ways far longer than other cultures simply because their agrarian lifestyle allowed them to settle and work the land near one another in high numbers in places like Bon Homme, Yankton, and Hutchinson Counties in southeast South Dakota; Edmunds, McPherson, Walworth and Campbell Counties in northwest South Dakota; McIntosh, Emmons, and Logan Counties in southcentral North Dakota; Pierce and McHenry Counties in northcentral North Dakota; Mercer, McLean, Sheridan, Oliver, and Dunn Counties in westcentral

North Dakota; and Morton, Stark, and Hettinger Counties west of the Missouri River; as well as the Provinces of Manitoba and Saskatchewan in Canada.

The sheer density of their settlement in those areas can still be felt today. It is not uncommon in the twenty-first century to walk the streets in Eureka, South Dakota; Ashley or other small towns in North Dakota, South Dakota, or Canada and hear the old German dialect spoken on the streets. Most of the octogenarians living in those areas started school unable to speak English and still prefer to carry on conversation with their peers in their German dialect. Many in my generation can still understand the dialect even if they aren't fluent in the language. For German-Russians and their descendants, language and identity are still linked, in part, because of the desire of the early settlers to maintain an ethnically intense environment. Staying under the radar allowed my German-Russian forbearers to focus on what mattered to them: language, religion, and the ability to own land and be self-sufficient.

Dr. William Sherman writes in *Prairie Mosaic: An Ethnic Atlas of Rural North Dakota,* "The tight-knit and local character of the typical North Dakota German communities tended to limit the horizons of their residents. Until the Second World War, German-Russians generally avoided higher education, state and national political office, and leadership in regional affairs."

War. My German ancestors who migrated to Russia in the early nineteenth century left their homes, in part, because of war. Recurrent wars in Europe created undue burdens on my people. Sons were drafted, crops and horses conscripted as well as a financial burden placed on them in carrying more than their share in the financial costs of war.

Dr. Adam Giesinger writes in, *From Catherine to Khrushchev*:

> When Russia's Catherine the Great (born a German Princess from the House of Anhalt Zerbst) invited German peasants to settle on

> her empty lands in 1763, her manifesto was a masterpiece of immigration propaganda, which became the cornerstone of Russia's colonization policy. Free transportation, freedom to settle anywhere, freedom to practice any trade or profession, generous allotments of free land to those who chose agriculture, free transportation, interest-free loans for ten years, freedom of customs duties for property brought in, freedom from taxes for five – thirty years, depending on the site of settlement, local self-government for those who established themselves in colonies, full freedom to practice their religion, freedom from military service, all privileges to be applicable also to their descendants, and finally, freedom to leave again if they found Russia unsuitable. What more could a prospective immigrant desire?

That initial invitation was to settle in colonies along the Volga River region. Thirty years later, Catherine's grandson, Alexander I, issued a similar manifesto to settle on virgin land in the Black Sea region. Giesinger continues,

> They came to the Black Sea region by the thousands, mainly from southwestern Germany, Württemberg, Baden, the Palatinate, the Hessian states and Alsace, where the Napoleonic wars had the greatest impact; but also from Hungary and from Poland, where Germans had settled earlier. The journey by boat and wagon and often on foot, took from two to five months and often meant wintering on the way. Arrived at the border the immigrants had to face a quarantine period and then live in primitive barracks for weeks or months before the settlement site was ready. The hardships of the journey and the first months in the new land were beyond the endurance of many. The mortality rate reached shocking proportions. Many families were almost wiped out and few reached the settlement sites intact.

By the time my agrarian ancestors arrived in the villages of Neudorf (1809) and Kassel (1814), two of the four original Glückstal Colonies settled as part of the Black Sea migration, they were ready to take on this new uncultivated steppe and make it bloom. When I study the histories of both these villages I am struck by the similarity to the pioneering experiences decades later in Dakota Territory. Smallpox, measles, blizzards, grasshoppers, crop failure, livestock epidemics, hailstorms, severe drought, early frost, balanced by the building of homes, churches, schools, community granaries, factories, wineries, steam mills, and as a benefit to their youngest citizens, an orphans fund. By the mid-nineteenth century, the Russian Steppe was producing wheat to feed the world. Vineyards and wineries were producing and selling wine to Europe's wealthiest, factories were on the cutting edge producing the latest farm machinery, the villages were thriving, and all was in harmony.

There really wasn't a reason to leave the Russian Steppe except for the undercurrent of envy and resentment of the special privileges granted the German colonists, their extensive land acquisitions, and their prosperity. It was the freeing of the serfs in 1861, new "Russification" measures such as use of the Russian language instead of German designed to assimilate the colonists into the Russian peasantry, and finally in January, 1874, a new military service law conscripting all medically fit male twenty-year-old Russian men to army service for six years that created incentive for the Germans in Russia to leave their beautiful villages and come to a new uncultivated land in North America.

Thirty years later, when the sons of those homesteading Germans-Russians in America were drafted to fight against German soldiers in France in World War I, it was a difficult reality. Now the war in Europe became local and personal. My people could no longer be isolated from the rest of the world. Many of those draftees only spoke German. They were charged with killing the only folks they could understand in that strange land of bunkers and tunnels and mustard gas. On the home front in

North and South Dakota, all German speakers were suspected of being German sympathizers. It wasn't enough to surrender your sons to fight, German-Russians were expected to communicate or worship only in English and to buy War Bonds to prove their loyalty to America.

Adding to their sorrow was the fact that communication with family left in South Russia was dwindling. Newspaper reports from the old country sounded ominous. Requests began to come for basic aid. Many homesteaders had lost touch with family and friends, but the German newspapers of the day, namely *Der Staats-Anzeiger*, *Eureka Rundschau*, and *Dakota Freie Presse* published letters from correspondents in the villages in South Russia. The letters tell of the closing of churches and schools following the Bolshevik Revolution, creating great educational and spiritual hardship. But things got worse, and the area became a world of terror fostered by Stalin's agrarian collectivization that left farmers stripped of not only their land and homes but unable to feed their families as the region faced mass starvation and for some, imprisonment lasting through the 1930s. Debra Marquart shares her family's milk letters in her essay, "Refusing Nostalgia," describing how, for that first generation of German-Russian homesteaders, the reality was the life they knew in Russia was destroyed, exuding such sobering and helpless sorrow that most simply couldn't talk about it. It would be decades before communication with relatives would begin again.

Most of the young men who survived World War I came home to the Dakota prairie to resume their agrarian life. They would be plagued with weak lungs for the rest of their lives, the result of repeated mustard gassings. Spanish influenza was raging and some came home to find their families cut in half by it. Others found their lungs could no longer take the cold and migrated once again. Some found their way to states of Washington and Oregon, where the milder climate allowed healthier living. Others made their way to California, most notably to the San Joaquin Valley area of Lodi, home of the Tokay Grape. In Lodi, they were able to grow grapes or vegetables or work in the wineries and canneries. It was another significant migration of the German-Russians.

For those who stayed in North and South Dakota, life resumed its old pace and flavor. The earliest homesteaders parceled out their land to descendants and moved to small towns, often bringing a cow and chickens with them. Instead of bumper wheat crops they grew large gardens, dug root cellars, canned what they could, dried and hung the rest in the attic and resumed life as they knew it on the edges of town.

The economy had its ups and downs; some families just couldn't make it and had to surrender their agrarian life and try to find work in town. Horses gave way to steam and later gasoline-powered machinery and roads began to improve.

When the economic crash of 1929 devastated the nation it was followed by years of drought and crop failure across the nation. Only farms that were not mortgaged and were able to grow their own food and buy hay for livestock seemed to be able survive without great hardship. The migrations from one continent to another, making do with what they had and employing creative problem-solving seemed to give the German-Russians in Dakota an edge in the survival game.

In an interview with my mother, Helen (Dockter) Just, I asked how her parents and their ten children fared during the Great Depression. She replied,

> We always lived frugally. Our farm was along Beaver Creek so we could water our gardens and grow all our own food. My brothers trapped and hunted. My dad had stored grain and hay that fed our livestock. I honestly didn't know there was a depression until my brothers, David and Otto, signed up for the Civilian Conservation Corp [CCC] and I enrolled in a WPA sponsored sewing class in Zeeland.

My mother added with some pride that they learned to create patterns, cut out fabric, and sewed the clothes for the boys in the CCC camps. Her finished products would be among the 2,078,451 garments sewn by trainees that Elwyn B. Robinson referenced on page 408 of *History of North Dakota.* My mother learned well and enjoyed a lifetime of sewing pleasure.

By the time the grandsons of the original homesteaders were drafted to serve in World War II, there was something of an acceptance of the reality that we were now German-Russian-Americans. Many draftees had already been away from home serving in the CCC and didn't see a problem fighting German speakers in Europe. For some, their first language as German speakers was an asset, and they were quickly channeled into service as interpreters of prisoners of war. Other German-Russian descendants served admirably in the Pacific Theater. For those who didn't come home, dreams were dashed and a new future had to be created for those left behind. Those who did come home had a new option: the GI Bill.

The GI Bill meant tuition for whatever kind of education a veteran wanted, and for many it meant leaving a life of agriculture to pursue careers in new areas of interest and geography. It was a period of a new generation of pioneering in parts of the country no German-Russian had previously ventured.

For the next two decades the Cold War prevented any communication with South Russia, but an interesting phenomenon took place in Germany after the war. Groups of Germans from Russia who were able to get to the west at the close of World War II created organizations to document their history and began hunting for American relatives.

By the mid1960s, German-Russian descendants in America were communicating with German-Russian descendants in Germany, resulting in collaboration by both sides, shared publishing endeavors, and a new era of research.

One of the first books in my German-Russian collection is a 1964 edition of Karl Stumpp's book titled, *The German-Russians,* which captures in text and photos the life and history in South

Russia in the early twentieth century. "Hard Working and Unassuming" is how Stumpp describes the people. There are photos of neat rows of homes in the villages with front gates and tree lined streets. The photographs of the people have a keen resemblance to my relatives in North and South Dakota.

With this first book of the many I would collect over the years of my research, I finally had a sense of the beautiful community my great-grandparents left to come to America. South Russia was no longer (in my mind) some short stop for my relatives on their way to the Promised Land. The stories and photos captured the beauty of the steppe, the strength of character and work ethic that carried my ancestors from continent to continent and passed to me and my generation. The responsibility continues as I try to share the stories of our people with the next generations.

In 1998 I joined North Dakota State University Libraries' Journey to the Homeland Tour sponsored by the Germans from Russia Heritage Collection (GRHC). My oldest daughter, Katharina, was able to take time from her studies in Berlin, Germany, to meet me in Odessa and to make a visit to the former villages of our ancestors. It was a life dream and a sobering experience to walk the streets they walked, find the homes they lived in, and visit the ruins of their beloved churches. There is an unmistakable similarity between the Russian Steppe and the Dakota prairie, making it almost feel like home. All Journey members experience a profound sense of appreciation for the raw courage and bravery of our great-grandparents who left their beautiful villages in South Russia to ensure for us the gift of freedom and life in a democracy.

Since then, there have been more journeys. Each trip to visit my ancestral villages in Russia, Germany, Poland, and France leaves me wanting to know more. Each time I walk a through a cemetery or sit in the beautiful sanctuary at St Andrew's, I hear the voices of those who came before me. Each time my grandchildren ask for a story about "our people," it is an opportunity to call forth and appreciate the memory of those who came before.

Was this long and enlightening path of research and preservation of my ethnic history in Grandpa Henry Dockter's grand plan when he gave me the photographs and told me their story?

I like to think so.

Bibliography

Sources are blended from all of the authors.

Aberle, George P. *From the Steppes to the Prairies: The Story of the Germans Settling in Russia on the Volga and Ukraine, also, the Germans Settling in the Banat, and the Bohemians in Crimea.* Bismarck: *Bismarck Tribune*, 1963.

Arends, Shirley Fischer. *The Central Dakota Germans: Their History, Language, and Culture.* Washington: Georgetown University Press, 1989.

Bridenthal, Renate. "Germans from Russia: The Political Network of a Double Diaspora," in The *Heimat Abroad: The Boundaries of Germanness*, ed. by Krista O'Donnell, Renate Bridenthal, and Nancy Reagin. Ann Arbor: University of Michigan Press, 2005.

_________. "Reaching Out: The Double Diaspora of Germans from Russia." Paper presented at The Heimat Abroad: The Boundaries of Germanness, New York University, 1999.

Burke, Peter. *Varieties of Cultural History.* Ithaca: Cornell University Press, 1997.

_________. *What is Cultural History.* Second Edition. Cambridge: Polity 2008.

Clark, Jessica. "Germans from Russia on the Northern Plains: An Oral History Project." PhD dissertation, North Dakota State University, 2010.

Dambach, Bob, Producer, with Ron Vossler, Writer. *The Germans from Russia: Children of the Steppe, Children of the Prairie.* Video, Fargo: Prairie Public, 1999.

Diede, Pauline Neher. *Homesteading on the Knife River Prairies.* Edited by Elizabeth Hampsten. Bismarck, ND: Germans from Russia Heritage Society, 1983.

Dunaway, David K. and Willa K. Baum. *Oral History: An Anthology.* New York: AltaMira Press, 1996.

Frisch, Michael. *A Shared Authority: Essays on the Craft and Meaning of Oral and Public History.* New York: State University of New Press, 1990.

Germans from Russia Heritage Collection, North Dakota State University, http://library.ndsu.edu/grhc.

Germans from Russia Heritage Society. https://www.grhs.org.

Giesinger, Adam. *From Catherine to Khrushchev: The Story of Russia's Germans.* Winnipeg: n.p., 1974.

Gjerde, Jon. *The Minds of the West: Ethnocultural Evolution in the Rural Middle West, 1830–1917.* Chapel Hill: University of North Carolina Press, 1999.

Height, Joseph S., Collector and Ed. *Folksongs of Our Forefathers: Liederbuch der Schwarzmeerdeutschen.* Bismarck: North Dakota Historical Society of Germans from Russia, 1978.

_________. *Homesteaders on the Steppe: Cultural History of the Evangelical-Lutheran Colonies in the Region of Odessa, 1804–1945.* Bismarck: North Dakota Historical Society of Germans from Russia, 1975.

_________. *Paradise on the Steppe: A Cultural History of the Kutschurgan, Beresan, and Liebenthal Colonists, 1804–1944.* Bismarck: North Dakota Historical Society of Germans from Russia, 1972.

Holt, Marilyn Irvin. *Children of the Western Plains: The Nineteenth-Century Experience.* Chicago: Ivan R. Dee, 2003.

"Hutmacher web page." https://library.ndsu.edu/grhc/history_culture/arch/hutmacher.html.

Koop, Michael H., Steven Ludwig, and Carolyn Torma. *German-Russian Folk Architecture in Southeastern South Dakota.* Vermillian: South Dakota State Historic Preservation Center, 1984.

Iseminger, Gordon L. "Are We Germans, or Russians, or Americans? The McIntosh County German-Russians During World War I." *North Dakota History* 82, no. 2 (Winter 2017): 3–16.

_________. "C. C. Becker: McIntosh County German-Russian Pioneer." *North Dakota History* 50, no. 3 (Summer 1983): 4–13.

_________. "The McIntosh County German-Russians: The First Fifty Years," North Dakota History 51, no. 3 (Summer 1984): 4–23.

Kloberdanz, Timothy J. "Cross-makers: German-Russian Folk Specialists of the Great Plains." PhD dissertation, Indiana University, 1986.

Langer, Lawrence L. *Holocaust Testimonies; The Ruins of Memory.* New Haven: Yale University Press, 1991.

Layman, Lenore. "Reticence in Oral History Interviews," *Oral History Review* 36, no. 2 (2009): 207–30.

Lubeke, Frederick C. "Ethnic Group Settlements on the Great Plains." *Western Historical Quarterly* 8 (1977): 405–30.

Martens, Steve. "Depression-Era Federal Relief Construction in North Dakota, 1931–1943." State Historical Society of North Dakota (NRHP October 2010). http://www.history.nd.gov/hp/PDFinfo/64501091FedReliefConstruction.pdf.

Martens, Steve C. and James W. Nelson. "From dust to dust . . .": The Temporal and Organic German-Russian Folk Architecture of Western North Dakota's Hutmacher Farmstead." Unpublished paper presented at the national meeting of Vernacular Architecture Forum, Lawrence, KS, April 11, 1996.

Martens, Steve and R.H.L.M. Ramsay. *Buildings of North Dakota.* Charlotte and London: University of Virginia Press, 2014. Excerpts available at www.SAH-Archipedia.org.

Miller, Michael M. *Researching the Germans from Russia: Annotated Bibliography of the Germans from Russia Heritage Collection.* Fargo: North Dakota Institute for Regional Studies, 1987.

Moon, David. *The American Steppes: The Unexpected RussianRoots of Great Plains Agriculture, 1870s–1930s.* Cambridge: Cambridge University Press, 2020.

North Star Chapter of Minnesota Germans from Russia. *Hollyhocks and Grasshoppers: Growing Up German from Russia in America.* Minneapolis: Mill City Press, 2013.

Perks, Robert and Alistair Thomson, eds. *The Oral History Reader.* London: Routledge, 2004.

Portelli, Alessandro. *The Order has been carried out: History, Memory, and Meaning of a Nazi Massacre in Rome.* New York: Palgrave, 2003.

Rath, George. *The Black Sea Germans in the Dakotas.* Freeman: Pine Hill Press, 1977.

Riney-Kehrberg, Pamela. *Childhood on the Farm: Work, Play, and the Coming of Age.* Lawrence, KS: University Press of Kansas, 2005.

Robinson, Elwyn B. *History of North Dakota.* Lincoln: University of Nebraska Press, 1966.

Sallet, Richard. *Russian-German Settlements in the United States.* Trans. by LaVern Rippley and Armand Bauer. Fargo, ND: North Dakota Institute for Regional Studies, 1974.

Schacter, Daniel L. *Searching for Memory: The Brain, the Mind, and the Past.* New York: Basic Books, 1996.

Sherman, William C., and Playford V. Thorson, Eds. *Plains Folk: North Dakota's Ethnic History*. Fargo: North Dakota Institute for Regional Studies, 1986.

Society of Architectural Historians. SAH Archipedia. https://sah-archipedia.org.

Stumpp, Karl. *The Emigration from Germany to Russia in the Years 1763 to 1862*. Lincoln: American Historical Association of Germans from Russia, 1982.

Thompson, Paul. *The Voice of the Past: Oral History*. Oxford University Press, 2000.

University of California—Berkely. "Living New Deal." https://livingnewdeal.org.

Vossler, Ron. *Dakota Kraut: A Memoir*. Fargo: Germans from Russia Heritage Collection, 2003.

__________. Prairie Spass: The Folk Humor of North Dakota's Germans from Russia." *North Dakota History* 66 (Summer/Fall 1999): 1–11.

Webb, Walter Prescott. *The Great Plains*. Boston: Ginn & Company, 1931.

West, Elliott. *Growing Up with the Country: Childhood Far Western Frontier*. Albuquerque: University of New Mexico Press, 1989.

Wishek, Nina Farley. *Along the Trails of Yesterday: A Story of McIntosh County*. Ashley, ND: *Ashley Tribune*, 1941.

Zelizer, Viviana. *Pricing the Priceless Child: The Changing Social Value of Children*. Princeton: Princeton University Press, 1985.

Zimmerman, Carle C. and Seth Russell, Eds. *Symposium on the Great Plains of North America*. Fargo: North Dakota Institute for Regional Studies, 1965.